HIGHER
AUTHORITY

OPERATE IN THE SUPERNATURAL POWER OF GOD
AND EXPOSE HELL'S PLOT TO DISTORT HUMANITY

HUGH DANIEL SMITH

DESTINY IMAGE® PUBLISHERS, INC.
P.O. Box 310, Shippensburg, PA 17257-0310

"Publishing cutting-edge prophetic resources to supernaturally empower the body of Christ"

This book and all other Destiny Image and Destiny Image Fiction books are available at Christian bookstores and distributors worldwide.

For more information on foreign distributors, call 717-532-3040.

Reach us on the Internet: www.destinyimage.com.

ISBN 13 TP: 978-0-7684-7731-3

ISBN 13 eBook: 978-0-7684-7732-0

For Worldwide Distribution, Printed in the U.S.A.

1 2 3 4 5 6 7 8 / 28 27 26 25 24

CONTENTS

FOREWORD

This is an exciting time to be alive, as we are watching the pages of Scripture come to life. The church is being positioned to advance the Kingdom of God in the earth as we partner with Heaven to birth revival and awakening. At the same time, we are not to be ignorant of satan's devices. There are demonic plans and agendas being pushed by forces of darkness to counter God's people. Through technology and artificial intelligence, there is a sinister plot afoot to infiltrate world systems with secular humanism and trans-humanism ideologies. In the coming years, we will see this unfold more and more.

God said these words to me: "You're going to see things that you've only seen in movies play out right before your eyes." As society seeks to gain access to the supernatural through various means, the Holy Spirit is—and will be—the power source and operating system of the believer.

The future is upon us now, and we must be prepared. The church has the opportunity to rise to the occasion to be on the ground floor of this technological advance and use it to advance God's plan in the world. Although the enemy has meant it for evil, believers everywhere will use technology—and even

artificial intelligence—to spread the message of the gospel. We can't afford to sit this one out. We must push back the darkness and be the light!

In this masterfully written book, *Higher Authority* by Bishop Hugh Smith, you will discover the enemy's devices and learn how to position yourself as a believer to be victorious in spite of evil agendas that are being devised in the earth. With the infusion of the Holy Spirit living within, you'll learn that you are a supernatural being called to affect change. Through the power of Jesus Christ, you are a new creation in Him. You will disrupt trends, schemes, and plans of wickedness in high places.

Through life experiences, expert biblical knowledge, and an undeniable anointing, Bishop Hugh Smith takes you on a journey to uncover your potential in Christ, break the confines of demonic chains, and walk in the fullness of your God-given purpose. This is a book that you will go back to again and again as fresh revelation and answers to your burning questions about yourself and your future are unearthed. As you read, prepare yourself to be transformed and experience God's supernatural enhancement for your life.

Joshua Giles
USA TODAY and ECPA Bestselling Author
Founder, Mantle Conference and Joshua Giles Ministries

THE WONDER
OF HUMAN POTENTIAL

THE DEPTHS AND HEIGHTS OF HUMANITY

"Do you mean we really are supposed to lock these people up in these small seclusion rooms with concrete floors and hard plastered walls, for the protection of themselves and others?"

This is the one question I found myself asking on many occasions while working at the Kalamazoo Regional State Psychiatric Hospital in the mid-80s. I felt disconcerted and deeply saddened at the depth of human dysfunction and brokenness I observed daily while employed there. During my tenure at the hospital, I was given the fortune—or misfortune, depending upon perspective—of witnessing human beings in both compromised and exalted states of being.

Imagine what it would be like to be so delusional that you truly believe you are the embodiment of some famous historical character. Or think about what it must feel like to have uncontrollable urges to consume your own excrement. Really consider the difficulty of being trapped in some mental

construct that has convinced you that people on the television are conspiring against you in some government-sponsored plot. Working at this institution provided me with the opportunity to witness all of this and more. It is these kinds of experiences and others that have led me to believe that the human being has the ability to rise to extraordinary heights, as well as sink to unimaginable lows.

During my early development, I was always mystified when contemplating the pain and violence human beings afflicted on each other. I could not prevent myself from asking questions:

- Why would somebody behave like that?

- Why did they abandon their children?

- How could she sell her offspring for her own temporal pleasure?

- How do you just take someone's life in cold blood?

- How do you pass a policy that you know will endanger the lives of many people?

- How can someone deny people their basic rights when it is in their power to grant them?

- Why would someone take advantage of the most vulnerable and least privileged among us?

These are a few of the questions that led me to pursue an understanding of the human essence and subsequently write this book.

This would be an empty, agonizing pursuit if this depth of brokenness was all there was to the human being. Fortunately, there is also greatness and a fascinating Christlike potential associated with the other side of the human spectrum. Consider Voyager 1, the robotic spacecraft that was launched in 1977 on a 40,000-year mission. Voyager 1 entered interstellar space nearly 35 years after its launch, streaking toward a star that is 17.6 light-years from earth. The team of scientists on the ground predicted that Voyager 1 would drift within 9.3 trillion miles of the star and swing by it to continue orbiting the center of our Milky Way galaxy. The ability to create, build, manage, and execute at this level is mind-bending and phenomenal. This is unequivocally a robust display of human exceptionalism. Consider what it would be like to activate and maximize all of your abilities. Or think about how it would feel to experience and enjoy a deeply meaningful and significant life.

When hearing of or witnessing human brilliance, I inwardly quake with enthusiasm, followed by a flood of questions:

- How were they able to perform with that level of skill and precision?

- How did Nelson Mandela survive 27 years of abuse in a South African prison and exit with a mind to forgive his captors?

- How did that person make $1 billion without a trail of blood behind them?

- What does real peace and tranquility feel like?

- How does pure joy affect the formation of personality?

- Is it really possible to unlock extraordinary abilities?

I believe the answers to these questions are embedded inside of the human being and revealed to those seeking understanding from our Creator.

ENAMORED BY HUMAN ENHANCEMENT

In 1974, science-fiction aficionados across America (and I count myself in that number) were fascinated by a new television series called *The Six Million Dollar Man*. The show was about a former astronaut, USAF Colonel Steve Austin, portrayed by Lee Majors, who was given bionic implants resulting in superhuman strength. Although I was only 11 years old when the show aired, I was absolutely enamored by the mere thought of human enhancement and the possibility of people functioning in concert with artificial technology.

Since that time, science and technology have significantly advanced in unimaginable ways. Today, human enhancement cannot be restricted to science-fiction theory, for in many ways it has already become science-fact. Human enhancement can be described as the natural, artificial, or technological alteration of the human body in order to enhance physical or mental capabilities. There are thousands of amputees in the world today whose damaged limbs have been replaced with prosthetics. Many others have recovered lost abilities by receiving artificial implants. And only God truly knows where all of this is going. Nevertheless, the experts in these disciplines are postulating a future that includes human augmentation and enhancements

by means of brain-computer interfaces, bionic parts, stem cell harvesting, and many other emerging technologies.

I really believe that the subject of human enhancement is indicative of humanity's innate knowledge that we are meant to be more than what we have become. However, while science continues its efforts to raise humanity by means of technology, I pray we remember the perfect man, Christ Jesus. The resurrected Christ has been enhanced by the glory of the Father and given the ability to do all things! And it is through Christ Jesus that believers also can be enhanced in ways that will make them appear supernatural. Together, in this book, let us explore the resurrected Christ and the process by which believers can be augmented by His person and parts.

According to the Scriptures, Jesus the Christ offered Himself to God as perfected humanity on behalf of fallen humanity. Christ's perfect being satisfied God's expectation of what He intended for His creation. Christ Jesus is the only person who has ever measured up to the true human blueprint. Therefore, it is only in Christ that the rest of humanity can be perfected. By virtue of His death, burial, resurrection, ascension, and rule, He completely fulfilled the Old Testament Levitical offerings, thereby making it possible for all humans to reach the standard of glory by redemptive enhancement through Christ.

BEAUTIFUL AND ASTONISHING

I remember like yesterday the deep joy and trepidation I felt after my first child was born in 1985. My wife Letha and I entered the wonderful and challenging world of parenting

at the tender ages of 21 and 22. From the moment our first daughter, Krystian, breathed her first breath, I knew we had been entrusted with the well-being of something more valuable and complex than any piece of technology ever created by a human being. In retrospect, it almost seems unthinkable for a novice or any untrained person to be given the weighty responsibility of caring for something so beautiful and astonishing as a human life. Think about it—people are required to meet a certain standard or criteria before they are permitted to manage things with far less value, yet the most precious lives are far too often placed in the hands of unprepared people.

At the time of this writing, Krystian is 38 years old, married to a wonderful husband, and she has three extraordinary sons of her own. Thanks be to God—Letha and I have managed to raise three beautiful daughters with the support of parents, family, and much prayer. To the tens of thousands of parents around the world who have successfully reared children: I commend you for your part in adding value to society. There are so many hard-working parents who have sacrificed much to help add doctors, attorneys, scientists, ministers, educators, entrepreneurs, or simply well-adjusted, quality people to our world.

The many years that have passed since the birth of my first daughter have not in any way diminished my love for, or interest in, human exceptionalism. As a matter of fact, I think my fire and curiosity have only intensified, and it is my sincere desire that you too will marvel and be in awe as we examine the human blueprint together.

After years of study and personal experiences, I am delighted to share some of the things I have learned regarding the human being. I urge you to consider this book a vehicle by which we

can travel together on this rewarding journey to increase our understanding and unleash the power of humanity.

Hugh Daniel Smith
Senior Pastor, Embassy Covenant Church International
Presiding Prelate, Jabula New Life Ministries International

CHAPTER 1

GOD'S DECREE
OF HUMAN ENHANCEMENT

FASCINATED BY "WONDER BEINGS"

From fictional superheroes to scientific human augmentation, from artificial intelligence to the search for alien life, our current generation is fascinated by "wonder beings" of one sort or another.

The highly anticipated film *Avengers: Endgame*, which featured superheroes from across the Marvel Cinematic Universe, grossed about $2.8 billion worldwide, and it was the highest-grossing film of all time from July 2019 to March 2021. *Avengers: Endgame* was the culmination of a 22-film superhero story that spanned more than a decade and had a colossal cultural impact around the globe.

Perhaps more significantly, the past several years have witnessed some shocking advances in real-life, scientific human enhancements. Many futurists, scientists, and thinkers are advocating the use of current and emerging technologies to augment human capabilities and enhance the human condition, with the ultimate goal of evolving into a "post-human" species. In fact, technology may soon alter the human body

and experience to the degree that the next big question of our time might become, "What is a human?" The very definition may be up for debate.

Stories and headlines about artificial intelligence have dominated recent news cycles, and AI is already having a notable impact on almost every major industry. Should we celebrate AI as one of the greatest human technological achievements thus far, or should we heed the doomsday warnings about an imminent machine-led apocalypse? What are we to make of all this?

In 2023, NASA also held its first public meeting on unidentified anomalous phenomena (UAP), more popularly known as UFOs; and for the first time, it has appointed a director of research on the topic. This move gives a level of credence to a subject of study that has long been relegated to the domain of marginalized conspiracy theorists.

Why are we, especially in this generation, so enamored by enhanced beings? I believe humanity is responding, in one way or another, to a divine decree that has gone out to the entire world. God is the only Original Thinker, and therefore, every thought that exists is either His original thought or some perversion of it. God has decreed human enhancement from the heavens, and the entire world is responding.

A DIVINE DECREE FROM THE HEAVENLY COUNCIL

According to the Scriptures, God rules by issuing divine decrees from the heavenly council, and these divine decrees shape both reality and destiny. The heavenly council facilitates the purposes of God and their fulfillment throughout the universe.

The notion of a divine council may be new for some believers, so it will be helpful to briefly offer a few biblical examples of this reality:

> The heavens praise your wonders, Lord, your faithfulness too, in **the assembly of the holy ones**. For who in the skies above can compare with the Lord? Who is like the Lord among the heavenly beings? In **the council of the holy ones** God is greatly feared; he is more awesome than all who surround him (**Psalm 89:5-7, NIV**).

> God has taken his place in **the divine council**; in the midst of the gods he holds judgment (**Psalm 82:1, ESV**).

> One day the members of **the heavenly court** came to present themselves before the Lord, and the Accuser, Satan, came with them (**Job 1:6, NLT**).

> Micaiah continued, "Therefore hear the word of the Lord: I saw the Lord sitting on his throne with all the multitudes of heaven standing around him on his right and on his left" (**1 Kings 22:19, NIV**).

> The sentence is by the decree of the watchers, the decision by the word of the holy ones, to the end that the living may know that the Most High rules the kingdom of men and gives it to whom he will and sets over it the lowliest of men (**Daniel 4:17, ESV**).

In these passages and others, the Bible affirms the existence of a divine council of heavenly beings that assist God

by carrying out His judgments and directives. God, being omnipotent, omniscient, and omnipresent, does not require assistance in governing all things. Yet, by His own choice, He has elected to involve created beings as co-rulers with Him. Imagine the profound impact finite beings experience when deliberating with the Most High on matters of life and reality. Being part of a council with exceptional human beings offers many benefits, but sitting at a council with the Almighty is truly mind-bending.

From this heavenly council, God issues divine decrees. A *decree* is "a formal and authoritative order, especially one having the force of law."[1] It can also be defined as a judicial decision, judgment, or order. In the realm of theology, a *decree* is "one of the eternal purposes of God, by which events are foreordained."[2] When God issues a decree, He is making a divine ruling on a particular matter.

For example, God decreed the vocation of the prophet Jeremiah before he was even born. When Jeremiah was still very young, God said to him, *"Before I formed you in the womb I knew you, before you were born I set you apart; I appointed you as a prophet to the nations"* (Jeremiah 1:5, NIV). In another place, David declares of God, *"For you created my inmost being; you knit me together in my mother's womb. …Your eyes saw my unformed body; all the days ordained for me were written in your book before one of them came to be"* (Psalm 139:13,16, NIV).

In our day, it is clear that God has made a decree concerning human enhancement. It is God's desire to see humanity augmented and empowered to fulfill their God-given destiny. His intent is for human beings, made in His image, to represent Him, embody His character, display His power, govern with His authority, and rule the earth in His stead. This decree

has been spread like a banner over the entire human race, and many are responding—either with the purity of God's original thought or with some distortion of it.

TRYING TO "GET BACK UP" SINCE THE FALL

The Bible says that God *"created human beings in his own image. In the image of God he created them; male and female he created them"* (Genesis 1:27, NLT). We as human beings were made in the image and likeness of God. This means that we carried and represented His nature, character, and power. We facilitated His vision and manifested it in the physical realm. We were His emissaries, His ambassadors, His delegates. We were the link between heaven and earth. We shone the light of God's image, and we were imbued with His authority to govern. It was God's intent to rule over the earth through His image—through humanity—and to cause every good thing to flourish under His wise and loving care.

From the beginning, we as human beings were designed and destined to rule with God. According to the Genesis account, when God created humanity, He blessed them, and He charged them to *"Be fruitful, and multiply, and replenish the earth, and subdue it: and have dominion over the fish of the sea, and over the fowl of the air, and over every living thing that moveth upon the earth"* (Genesis 1:28, KJV). Some have called this assignment from God the "Dominion Mandate"—the divine command to sovereignly govern the earth in God's stead.

Because Adam and Eve were made in God's image and enjoyed perfect union with Him, many have speculated about

what they may have been capable of—traveling at the speed of thought, accessing vast amounts of knowledge, tapping into incredible spiritual insight, co-creating with God, ruling over all created beings on the earth, etc. Heaven and earth were united in the Garden of Eden, and with God, anything was possible.

We know from the descriptions and effects of the Tree of Life and the Tree of the Knowledge of Good and Evil that the fruits of the trees opened up spiritual dimensions. In the initial dispensation, Adam and Eve's consumption of fruit extended beyond physical nourishment, intertwining with spiritual enlightenment. The Garden's trees, including the Tree of Life and the Tree of the Knowledge of Good and Evil, served as gateways to various dimensions. Their meals were both sustenance for the body and nourishment for the spirit—a harmonious blend of natural and spiritual food. In this state, spiritual enlightenment seamlessly accompanied the pleasure of a favorite meal, eliminating the need for separate practices like prayer and fasting.

Adam and Eve might have effortlessly moved between Kingdom dimensions as they partook of the fruit from the approved trees. Remember, after they ate from the Tree of the Knowledge of Good and Evil, a dimensional door of death opened, plummeting the entire human family into sin and death. At any rate, the unity between spiritual and physical food is no longer. Jesus emphasized this separation between physical sustenance and spiritual nourishment when He said, "*Man shall not live on bread alone, but on every word that comes from the mouth of God*" (Matthew 4:4, NIV). (Despite this separation, it is possible to restore the sacredness of mealtime: spiritual and physical nourishment can be reunited by pronouncing a

proper blessing and engaging in stimulating spiritual conversation during meals.)

We also know that when Christ came as the Second Adam, the image of the invisible God, He had power to heal the sick, raise the dead, cast out demons, multiply food, turn water into wine, walk on water, command the wind, and discern the thoughts of the people around Him. This likely indicates what God originally intended for the First Adam, and perhaps it provides some insight into what humanity was initially capable of. Whatever the case, it is certainly true that we were (and are) "*fearfully and wonderfully made*" (Psalm 139:14, NIV).

When we disobeyed God's instructions in the Garden, the image of God in us was distorted, and our original glory and capacity were severely diminished and degraded. (To this day, some suggest that we only use small percentages of our brains' capacities and that we use an even smaller percentage of the coding power of our DNA.) It truly was a "Fall" in every meaningful sense of the word, and ever since that Fall, humanity has been attempting to get back up again.

We sense intuitively that we were made for more—that we are so much more than what we have become. We know that we were intended to be glorious beings full of power and wonder, and the disparity between "what is" and "what should be" can create within us a nagging cognitive dissonance. We are not wired to deal with sickness, death, and defeat. We instinctively search for a better reality. We are kings and queens in exile, and in one way or another, we are trying to reassert our right to rule.

Christ came to restore us back to our rightful place as the image bearers of God. He is the perfect human—the blueprint

for what God always intended for humanity—and we are instructed to *"mark the perfect man"* (Psalm 37:37, KJV). As believers in Christ, we are now actively being transformed and conformed to His image, and we are reclaiming our right to rule as God's ambassadors in the earth. *"For whom he did foreknow, he also did predestinate to be conformed to the image of his Son, that he might be the firstborn among many brethren"* (Romans 8:29, KJV). We have taken off the old humanity and we have put on the new, enhanced humanity, *"which is renewed in knowledge after the image of him that created him"* (Colossians 3:10, KJV).

The more we see Christ, the more we are transformed into His image and the more power we have to embrace our enhanced humanity. For as we behold Him, we are being *"transformed into the same image from one degree of glory to another"* (2 Corinthians 3:18, ESV), and *"in him we live, and move, and have our being"* (Acts 17:28, KJV).

THE LADDER BETWEEN HEAVEN AND EARTH

Human beings were created to serve as conduits between heaven and earth. We have the capacity through our human spirits to connect with God and the entire spirit world. Our souls give us the wherewithal to be self-conscious and aware of other people. And it is through our bodies that we are granted access to this physical domain.

A fully functional human being can be compared to a ladder, with respect to the kind of service he or she renders. The primary purpose of a ladder is to give individuals trapped at

lower levels access to things at higher levels. The human being has been divinely designed as a trans-dimensional being with access to three worlds. God's original intent is for the human to have communion with Himself and the spirit world by means of the human spirit, communion with the internal social world of humanity by means of the human soul, and communion with the physical world by means of the human body.

Jesus provides us with a wonderful example of the human being functioning like a ladder, giving people access to higher levels and dimensions, in His important interview with a man named Nathanael:

> *The next day Jesus decided to leave for Galilee. Finding Philip, he said to him, "Follow me."*
>
> *Philip, like Andrew and Peter, was from the town of Bethsaida. Philip found Nathanael and told him, "We have found the one Moses wrote about in the Law, and about whom the prophets also wrote—Jesus of Nazareth, the son of Joseph."*
>
> *"Nazareth! Can anything good come from there?" Nathanael asked.*
>
> *"Come and see," said Philip.*
>
> *When Jesus saw Nathanael approaching, he said of him, "Here truly is an Israelite in whom there is no deceit."*
>
> *"How do you know me?" Nathanael asked.*
>
> *Jesus answered, "I saw you while you were still under the fig tree before Philip called you."*
>
> *Then Nathanael declared, "Rabbi, you are the Son of God; you are the king of Israel."*

Jesus said, "You believe because I told you I saw you under the fig tree. You will see greater things than that." He then added, "Very truly I tell you, you will see 'heaven open, and the angels of God ascending and descending on' the Son of Man" (**John 1:43-51, NIV**).

In the above passage, Jesus fulfilled the Old Testament account of Jacob's ladder by identifying Himself as the ladder that stood between heaven and earth with angels ascending and descending on Him. His spiritual and soulish intelligence enabled Him to see and know the disciples He would select, without even having a face-to-face physical encounter with them. I believe Jesus was capable of calling and interacting with His would-be disciples through spiritual senses long before He saw them with natural eyes.

Before calling His disciples, Jesus spent the entire night in prayer: "*In these days he went out to the mountain to pray, and all night he continued in prayer to God. And when day came, he called his disciples and chose from them twelve, whom he named apostles*" (Luke 6:12-13, ESV). Using a little deductive reasoning, it seems plausible that Jesus identified and called His future disciples to Him while praying in the Spirit. The Bible provides ample evidence that all things originate in the invisible realm before manifesting in the physical. Jesus' short invitation to the would-be disciples to follow Him likely indicates the spiritual connection He had already established with them during His night of prayer.

Having this kind of dimensional insight today could save many employers from the grievous mistake of hiring the wrong people. Of even greater import, this insight could save

thousands from marrying or being joined to the wrong person. People who are unaware of their true spiritual makeup can only observe the outward appearance of the people they interact with, but God and people who are enlightened by Him can see into the inward parts of humanity. The old adage is true: you cannot judge a book by its cover. Needless to say, Jesus knew the men He was interviewing even better than they knew themselves.

In this passage, Jesus also emphatically claimed to be the way to the living God. As the proverbial ladder standing between earth and heaven, Jesus could access dimensions beyond and heaven above. Today, angels continue this same practice in their service to believers. They are eager and ready to ascend and descend on all who position themselves as conduits, gateways, portals, or ladders to heaven.

Consider Jacob's discovery of the gate of heaven while on his way to Harran:

> Jacob left Beersheba and set out for Harran. When he reached a certain place, he stopped for the night because the sun had set. Taking one of the stones there, he put it under his head and lay down to sleep. He had a dream in which he saw a stairway resting on the earth, with its top reaching to heaven, and the angels of God were ascending and descending on it. There above it stood the Lord, and he said: "I am the Lord, the God of your father Abraham and the God of Isaac. I will give you and your descendants the land on which you are lying. Your descendants will be like the dust of the earth, and you will spread out to the west and to the east, to the north and to the

south. All peoples on earth will be blessed through you and your offspring. I am with you and will watch over you wherever you go, and I will bring you back to this land. I will not leave you until I have done what I have promised you."

When Jacob awoke from his sleep, he thought, "Surely the Lord is in this place, and I was not aware of it." He was afraid and said, "How awesome is this place! This is none other than the house of God; this is the gate of heaven" (**Genesis 28:10-17, NIV**).

Jesus fulfilled Jacob's ladder by using His entire being as a gateway. His ministry was characterized by communicating humanity's needs to the heavens and thereafter meeting those needs by procuring and transmitting heaven's resources to the earth.

In antiquity, the term *gate* or *gateway* held a significant place in the minds of the people, not only in the defense of a city but also in the public economy. The gate represented the city council or strategic plans, the court or judicial affairs, and the marketplace or business sector. Our challenge today is to move from fear-based and shame-based, powerless religion to centers that empower the "gifted and called" to become gateways of spiritual access.

A CRITICAL MOMENT IN HISTORY

In this end time, there is a concentrated focus on human enhancements because God is actively restoring human beings

to their former glory. Before Jesus went to the cross, He prayed, *"now, Father, glorify me in your presence with the glory I had with you before the world began"* (John 17:5, NIV). We, too, are in Christ, looking for the day of glory, and one day, we will receive the full glorification that God has allocated for us. But we are also being glorified now, for Christ will have His *"glorious church"* (Ephesians 5:27, KJV).

We as believers are being enhanced to fulfill God's Kingdom agenda in the earth. We are being given supernatural powers and abilities so that we can exercise dominion over creation— so that we can displace the enemy, advance the Kingdom, and establish God's rule in the earth. But once again, God's decree of human enhancement has been released over the entire world, and though He has a plan to enhance humanity through Christ, others are attempting to enhance humanity by their own means. In one way or another, God's decree is affecting the entire human race.

The Kingdom of God is ramping up, and so is the kingdom of darkness. God is enhancing His people, and so is the enemy. There are two big agendas for the earth, and both sides are currently amassing power and preparing for a final conflict.

ASCENSION GIFTS MUST EQUIP THE SAINTS <u>NOW</u>

It is evident from the heightened culture wars of our time that a clash of kingdoms is imminent. The world is becoming increasingly polarized, and people have embraced drastically different visions of human society. In many ways, the boundary lines

are being drawn between God's Kingdom and the kingdom of the enemy.

Now more than ever, it is absolutely imperative that ascension gifts equip the saints for what is to come. The apostle Paul spoke of this in his letter to the Ephesians:

> *And He Himself gave some to be apostles, some prophets, some evangelists, and some pastors and teachers, for the equipping of the saints for the work of ministry, for the edifying of the body of Christ, till we all come to the unity of the faith and of the knowledge of the Son of God, to a perfect man, to the measure of the stature of the fullness of Christ; that we should no longer be children, tossed to and fro and carried about with every wind of doctrine, by the trickery of men, in the cunning craftiness of deceitful plotting, but, speaking the truth in love, may grow up in all things into Him who is the head—Christ—from whom the whole body, joined and knit together by what every joint supplies, according to the effective working by which every part does its share, causes growth of the body for the edifying of itself in love* (**Ephesians 4:11-16, NKJV**).

I'm confident that if the "gifted and called" of humanity receive the proper nurture, they will emerge as the shining lights they were designed to be. Unfortunately, far too many are left to fend for themselves—protracting or lengthening a process of development that could be accomplished at a much faster rate. "Nurture" refers to the influence of milieu and environmental conditions that impact who we are or who we can

become. Without adequate and intentional nurture, the most gifted among us may be sentenced to live and die in the prison of unrealized potential.

In several New Testament passages, the apostle Paul acknowledges the vital role that nurture plays in the development of the believer. Consider what he says to the Galatians: *"My dear children, for whom I am again in the pains of childbirth until Christ is formed in you"* (Galatians 4:19, NIV). Paul corroborates the power of nurture by using the term *formed* (from the Greek word *morphe*) in the above text. He is essentially saying that he, like a woman in travail, has created a "womb" or birthing-like environment through which he will produce Christ in his spiritual offspring. I think it is critical that we note that his ultimate objective was never for believers to sit in pews and watch the minister work the works of God alone, but it was for them to share in this powerful work after being transformed into the image of Christ.

Like a caterpillar that forms a chrysalis and morphs into a butterfly, Paul's apostolic ministry serves as a chrysalis of some sort that catalyzes metamorphosis. The apostle's dedication to the nurturing process is evident in his commitment to travailing until Christ is formed in his children of faith. Imagine what it would be like if every believer and every local church was a gateway to heaven, an authentic house of God. If this were so, the Church would have no problems in fulfilling her mission to reveal Christ to the world.

In this critical time, the ascension gifts within the Body of Christ must do the work of equipping the people of God so that they can become the enhanced humanity that God intends them to be. I pray that our Lord raises up apostles, prophets, evangelists, pastors, and teachers who will accurately judge

success in ministry by the quality of the Christ in those souls entrusted to their care. May our Lord raise up leaders who will nurture and travail until Christ is formed in God's people and their God-given potential becomes a reality.

The Spirit of the Lord said that He is raising spiritual giants—transformed and empowered by Christ to influence and impact cities and nations for the glory of God. We will witness boot camp-like trainings for God's people happening globally, preparing them for the impending clash between the Kingdom of Light and the kingdom of darkness.

If we fail in this charge, the ramifications could be devastating. If we fail to enhance believers with the power of God right now, we may lose an entire generation. There will be a strong delusion that comes, and they will embrace the other side. If we are not prepared for the kingdom clash that is coming, then we will suffer the shame of reproach, and there may be a negative impact for generations. Entire nations may become secularized communities devoid of the power of God.

In the rest of this book, we will highlight the two distinct paths to enhanced humanity—one through Christ and the other through transhumanism—and we will teach you how to become enhanced through Christ. We may only have a couple years to get everyone enhanced, so we must act with a sense of urgency. Like the military, ascension gifts in the Body of Christ must equip, train, and prepare the people of God for the impending conflict. The time is now!

NOTES

1. Dictionary.com, s.v. "Decree," https://www.dictionary.com/browse/decree.

2. Ibid.

TWO PATHS
TO AN ENHANCED HUMANITY

THE DAYS OF NOAH HAVE RETURNED

When speaking of His Second Coming, Jesus said, *"As it was in the days of Noah, so it will be at the coming of the Son of Man"* (Matthew 24:37, NIV). He was referring to the fact that people were *"eating and drinking, marrying and giving in marriage, up to the day Noah entered the ark; and they knew nothing about what would happen until the flood came and took them all away"* (Matthew 24:38-39, NIV). For them, life was going on as normal, and they were oblivious to the divine judgment that was coming upon them.

In more ways than one, the days of Noah have truly returned. Consider the state of the world in Noah's time:

> *When human beings began to increase in number on the earth and daughters were born to them, the sons of God saw that the daughters of humans were beautiful, and they married any of them they chose. Then the Lord said, "My Spirit will not contend with humans forever, for they are mortal; their days will be a hundred and twenty years."*

> *The Nephilim were on the earth in those days—and also afterward—when the sons of God went to the daughters of humans and had children by them. They were the heroes of old, men of renown.*
>
> *The Lord saw how great the wickedness of the human race had become on the earth, and that every inclination of the thoughts of the human heart was only evil all the time. The Lord regretted that he had made human beings on the earth, and his heart was deeply troubled. So the Lord said, "I will wipe from the face of the earth the human race I have created—and with them the animals, the birds and the creatures that move along the ground—for I regret that I have made them." But Noah found favor in the eyes of the Lord* (**Genesis 6:1-8, NIV**).

Other than the generalized violence and corruption mentioned later on in this chapter of Scripture, the one egregious sin that is prominently highlighted is the sexual intercourse between the "sons of God" and the "daughters of humans." According to this passage, many scholars suggest that fallen angelic beings were actually cross-breeding with human women and producing a race of Nephilim—enhanced human beings who became the "heroes of old, men of renown."

In various biblical passages, it is noted that God appointed angels as guardians over nations, forming a heavenly council where decisions impacting earth were made. This system thrived when these angels adhered to God's authority. However, after lucifer's insurrection, the angels who followed him tainted their assigned nations with malevolent influences, introducing premature and distorted technologies and ideologies. This

disruption is linked to the diverse religions, beliefs, and varying levels of advancement worldwide. Deuteronomy 32:8 (NLT) underscores God's role in assigning lands to nations through His heavenly court: *"When the Most High assigned lands to the nations, when he divided up the human race, he established the boundaries of the peoples according to the number in his heavenly court."* Daniel 10 provides us with a window into this spiritual reality, with its references to Michael—the angelic prince of Israel—and his warfare against the angelic prince of Persia. (The angelic prince of Greece is also mentioned.) The psalms also provide support for this understanding of angels' influence on nations.

As we know, human beings were originally made in the image and likeness of God, and this "hacking" of the human identity by fallen angelic beings was corrupting the very definition of what it meant to be a human being. The human genetic code itself was being tampered with, and God no longer recognized His creation. A hybrid race of creatures was being produced, and like a pandemic it was spreading and corrupting the entire world. It was this corruption that prompted God to wipe the slate clean and cleanse the earth with a flood. God had to hit the "reset button" because creation itself had to be fundamentally renewed.

Noah found favor in God's sight because he was *"a righteous man, blameless among the people of his time, and he walked faithfully with God"* (Genesis 6:9, NIV). Given the broader context of the chapter, it is highly possible that Noah was considered "blameless among the people of his time" because he was still a "pure human." The King James Version says he was "perfect in his generations." His genetic code was still intact because

his family line had not been corrupted by sexual relations with fallen angelic beings.

In our day, many are once again pursuing an enhanced humanity, and the very definition of a human being may soon be up for discussion. The "men of renown" may return as humanity is hacked, augmented, and given hybrid abilities. Later in this chapter, we will discuss some specific scientific enhancements that are currently being explored.

THERE HAVE ALWAYS BEEN TWO PATHS TO ENHANCEMENT

Before we highlight the specific enhancements that are on the table in our day, we must first note that, in some ways, this reality is not new. Throughout human history, there have always been two distinct paths to enhancement.

When lucifer fell from heaven, his tail drawing with him "*a third of the stars*" (Revelation 12:4, NIV), he and his demonic cohorts "*kept not their first estate*" (Jude 6, KJV). They left their original property, jurisdiction, and personhood. They were enshrouded in darkness, and they tapped into a so-called wisdom that "*does not come down from heaven but is earthly, unspiritual, demonic*" (James 3:15, NIV). This "wisdom" is a twisted perversion of the wisdom of God, and these demonic entities have been attempting to use their powers in their fallen, demonic realm.

When the serpent showed up in the Garden to tempt the woman to eat of the forbidden fruit, he said to her, "*God knows*

that when you eat from it your eyes will be opened, and you will be like God, knowing good and evil" (Genesis 3:5, NIV). Adam and Eve were enticed by a promise of enhancement from the enemy, and indeed, *"the eyes of both of them were opened"* (Genesis 3:7, NIV), but only to their own nakedness. The tragic irony is that, prior to their sin, they were already made in the image and likeness of God and had unhindered access to the Tree of Life, as well as all the other trees of the Garden. They had all the enhancement that they would ever need in the presence of God, but they attempted to gain it by other means.

Several generations later, fallen humanity said, *"Come, let us build ourselves a city, with a tower that reaches to the heavens, so that we may make a name for ourselves; otherwise we will be scattered over the face of the whole earth"* (Genesis 11:4, NIV). The Tower of Babel was more than a simple physical structure. It was constructed as a ziggurat-style temple, and it was an attempt to pierce into the heavens by the power of human ingenuity. The name *Babel* means "the gate of god" or "the gate of heaven." It also sounds like the Hebrew word *balal*, which means "to confuse," and the author of Genesis makes use of this wordplay in the story.

The builders of this tower were trying to access and dominate the spirit realm for their own purposes. Some also believe that this was Nimrod's attempt to vigorously defy God's judgment by building a structure too high for floodwaters to reach. Babel was later consolidated into the Babylonian Empire that destroyed Jerusalem and took the Israelites into captivity, and it resurfaces again as eschatological Babylon in the book of Revelation, where it finally falls into utter ruin.

The spirit of Babylon, then and now, is embodied by globalization, human autonomy, and defiance toward God. It

manifests in the rising aspirations for a New World Order encompassing a global currency, technocratic governance, pervasive surveillance, forced assimilation, and an antichrist figure—a longstanding intent of the spirit of Babylon.

Standing in sharp contrast to the story of Babel is the story of Bethel, which we referenced in the previous chapter of this book:

> *Jacob left Beersheba and set out for Harran. When he reached a certain place, he stopped for the night because the sun had set. Taking one of the stones there, he put it under his head and lay down to sleep. He had a dream in which he saw a stairway resting on the earth, with its top reaching to heaven, and the angels of God were ascending and descending on it. There above it stood the Lord, and he said: "I am the Lord, the God of your father Abraham and the God of Isaac. I will give you and your descendants the land on which you are lying. Your descendants will be like the dust of the earth, and you will spread out to the west and to the east, to the north and to the south. All peoples on earth will be blessed through you and your offspring. I am with you and will watch over you wherever you go, and I will bring you back to this land. I will not leave you until I have done what I have promised you."*
>
> *When Jacob awoke from his sleep, he thought, "Surely the Lord is in this place, and I was not aware of it." He was afraid and said, "How awesome is this place! This is none other than the house of God; this is the gate of heaven"* (**Genesis 28:10-17, NIV**).

Jacob, grandson of Abraham, is visited by God in a dream, and he sees a stairway that connects the heavens and the earth, with Yahweh standing above it and angels ascending and descending upon it. When he awakes, he calls the place *Bethel*, which means "house of God," for he calls this place "the gate of heaven." In the Gospel of John, Jesus says to Nathanael, "*Very truly I tell you, you will see 'heaven open, and the angels of God ascending and descending on' the Son of Man*" (John 1:51, NIV). God always intended to reunite heaven and earth—and to do so through humanity—but while Nimrod and his group were trying to "hack" their way into the heavenly realms, God was preparing to open the heavens to His covenant people in His own way.

Later on in the biblical story, Aaron threw down his staff in front of Pharaoh and his officials and the staff became a snake. "*Pharaoh then summoned wise men and sorcerers, and the Egyptian magicians also did the same things by their secret arts: Each one threw down his staff and it became a snake. But Aaron's staff swallowed up their staffs*" (Exodus 7:11-12, NIV). The pagan sorcerers were able to mimic God's power for a moment, but Aaron's staff swallowed up their staffs, demonstrating the superiority of God's power. The sorcerers were also able to mimic the plague of blood, but as the plagues on Egypt continued, they eventually admitted to Pharaoh, "*This is the finger of God*" (Exodus 8:19, NIV).

The Bible acknowledges the reality of spiritual practices that function outside of God's will and purpose, and for this reason, God instructs His people in Deuteronomy 18:10-11 (NIV), "*Let no one be found among you who sacrifices their son or daughter in the fire, who practices divination or sorcery,*

interprets omens, engages in witchcraft, or casts spells, or who is a medium or spiritist or who consults the dead."

Witchcraft may be a reality, but "Christ craft" is infinitely superior, and the Bible speaks of "craftsmen" who will *"throw down these horns of the nations who lifted up their horns against the land of Judah to scatter its people"* (Zechariah 1:21, NIV). A craftsman is a skilled, mature, and influential individual. In the era of spiritual growth, there will arise experts capable of extraordinary feats through their mastery of spiritual principles. Kingdom expertise will be instrumental in neutralizing the powers of darkness and fulfilling God's will on earth—aligning with the divine order in heaven.

Rather than immediately celebrating individuals' achievements, it is crucial to discern the source of their success. In our time, some may accomplish remarkable feats through demonic influence. Unfortunately, the pursuit of success, fame, and wealth has led some to compromise their integrity, trading their souls for worldly gains. Yet as Jesus questioned, what is the value of gaining the whole world if it costs one's soul? The human soul is invaluable, far surpassing the wealth of this world, and no temporary advancement is worth the eternal consequences of selling one's soul. Moreover, God's gift and purpose outweigh anything the evil one could offer.

Jesus said, *"Very truly I tell you, I am the gate for the sheep"* (John 10:7, NIV), the only legitimate entry point. However, He also called attention to the thieves and robbers—those who climb in *"by some other way"* (John 10:1, NIV). These have always been the two paths to human enhancement—the path of God and the path of human (and demonic) ingenuity. Only one is legitimate, and only one will ultimately succeed.

TRANSHUMANISM—HUMAN ENHANCEMENT THROUGH SCIENCE AND TECHNOLOGY

Transhumanism is "the belief or theory that the human race can evolve beyond its current physical and mental limitations, especially by means of science and technology."[1]

According to *Britannica, transhumanism* is a:

> Philosophical and scientific movement that advocates the use of current and emerging technologies—such as genetic engineering, cryonics, artificial intelligence (AI), and nanotechnology—to augment human capabilities and improve the human condition. Transhumanists envision a future in which the responsible application of such technologies enables humans to slow, reverse, or eliminate the aging process, to achieve corresponding increases in human life spans, and to enhance human cognitive and sensory capacities. The movement proposes that humans with augmented capabilities will evolve into an enhanced species that transcends humanity—the "posthuman."[2]

Notably, some are also combining this philosophy with a form of spirituality:

> In *The Physics of Immortality* (1994), for example, the American physicist Frank Tipler borrowed from the French Jesuit theologian and paleontologist Pierre Teilhard de Chardin's Omega point theory—which

proposes that evolution is converging toward a final unity—to present a concept of God as a cosmic computerized intelligence that is equivalent to the Omega. When the Omega point is reached, everyone will experience a computational resurrection into immortality.[3]

If this isn't the Tower of Babel all over again, then what is?

We must note, however, that technology itself is neutral—neither good nor evil—and many technological advancements have drastically improved the human condition. Even with many of the technologies that are currently being explored, there are perhaps many potential benefits. However, a tool for one person is a weapon for another, and the question we must continually ask ourselves is, "How will this technology be used?" There is a great need for informed, ethical regulation when it comes to emerging technologies, but right now, technological advancement is far outpacing our ability to adequately regulate it. Thus, we are in uncharted territory.

We must consider the ethical boundary lines of these technologies. When have we crossed the line? When are we going beyond human enhancement and actively distorting God's intent for creation? When are we tampering with His image in the earth—as they were in the days of Noah? When are we corrupting God's good designs for us?

CERN's Large Hadron Collider is the world's largest and most powerful particle accelerator, and in 2004, CERN unveiled a 2-meter statue of an Indian god known as Lord Shiva the Destroyer, one of the members of the Hindu trinity. According to CERN:

In the Hindu religion, this form of the dancing Lord Shiva is known as the Nataraj and symbolises Shakti, or life force. As a plaque alongside the statue explains, the belief is that Lord Shiva danced the Universe into existence, motivates it, and will eventually extinguish it. Carl Sagan drew the metaphor between the cosmic dance of the Nataraj and the modern study of the "cosmic dance" of subatomic particles.[4]

To what extent are we mingling science and spirituality? To what extent are we attempting to connect to another realm by means of physics or computers? To what extent are some modern-day scientists acting as the priests of an altogether different kind of religion? We must ask these critical questions—now more than ever.

EMERGING TECHNOLOGIES FOR HUMAN ENHANCEMENT

In this section, we will draw attention to several of the emerging technologies that are being designed for human enhancement. However, there are two important caveats before we begin:

1. We are not necessarily making a value judgment in each of these cases. Once again, technology itself is neither good nor evil. It all depends on how it is used. However, it is highly possible that many of these technologies may cross (or already are crossing) ethical boundary lines in one way or another.

2. We do not intend to provide exhaustive descriptions or analyses of each technology. Each is a field of study on its own. We simply intend to offer brief descriptions that will help us to open our eyes to what is currently happening in this arena.

With that, let us take a look at several emerging technologies that may advance the possibilities of transhumanism:

Genome Editing (Gene Editing)

Genome editing (also called gene editing) is a group of technologies that give scientists the ability to change an organism's DNA. These technologies allow genetic material to be added, removed, or altered at particular locations in the genome. Several approaches to genome editing have been developed. A well-known one is called CRISPR-Cas9, which is short for clustered regularly interspaced short palindromic repeats and CRISPR-associated protein 9. The CRISPR-Cas9 system has generated a lot of excitement in the scientific community because it is faster, cheaper, more accurate, and more efficient than other genome editing methods.[5]

According to the National Human Genome Research Institute, CRISPR is "a technology that research scientists use to selectively modify the DNA of living organisms. CRISPR was adapted for use in the laboratory from naturally occurring genome editing systems found in bacteria."[6] Gene editing holds

the potential to modify the appearance and abilities of human beings.

Gene Doping

According to *Britannica, gene doping* is the:

> Use of substances or techniques to manipulate cells or genes in order to improve athletic performance. Since the latter half of the 20th century, the manipulation of human genes has formed an important area of biomedical research, with much effort focused in particular on refining gene therapy for the treatment of diseases such as cystic fibrosis and anemia. In the early 21st century, however, members of the international sports community became concerned that athletes seeking to gain physical advantage in competition would abuse gene therapy and similar technologies.[7]

Neuralink Chip

Neuralink is a startup company from billionaire entrepreneur Elon Musk. Neuralink's mission is to "create a generalized brain interface to restore autonomy to those with unmet medical needs today and unlock human potential tomorrow." The company believes that "brain-computer interfaces have the potential to change lives for the better" and they want to "bring this technology from the lab into peoples' homes."

Their "brain-computer interface is fully implantable, cosmetically invisible, and designed to let you control a computer or mobile device anywhere you go. Advanced, custom, low-power chips and electronics process neural signals, transmitting them wirelessly to the Neuralink Application, which decodes the data stream into actions and intents."[8] In other words, this electronic chip that is inserted into the brain would allow people to communicate with and operate computers simply by thinking.

Brain-computer interfaces have the potential to revolutionize the learning process by directly downloading vast amounts of information into the human brain.

Cryonics

According to the Cryonics Institute:

> Cryonics involves cooling a recently deceased person to liquid nitrogen temperatures in order to keep the body preserved indefinitely. Our goal is to keep the patient preserved until future science may be able to repair or replace vital tissues and ultimately revive the patient. It might seem like an impossible goal to "revive" a "dead" person. However, "dying" is a process rather than an event. A majority of the body's tissues remain intact at a cellular level even after the heart stops beating. The goal of cryonics is to halt that process as quickly as possible after legal death, giving future physicians the best possible chance of reviving the patient. This may include repairing or

replacing damaged tissues and even entire organs using advanced computer systems, nanotechnology and medical equipment and procedures. While no one can be sure about the path of future technology, we believe that this could happen in a future where our lifespans can be significantly, even radically, extended.[9]

This organization is actively exploring and pursuing the prospect of immortality through scientific means.

Nanotechnology

According to the CDC:

Nanotechnology is the manipulation of matter on a near-atomic scale to produce new structures, materials and devices. The technology promises scientific advancement in many sectors such as medicine, consumer products, energy, materials, and manufacturing. Nanotechnology refers to engineered structures, devices, and systems. Nanomaterials have a length scale between 1 and 100 nanometers. At this size, materials begin to exhibit unique properties that affect physical, chemical, and biological behavior. Researching, developing, and utilizing these properties is at the heart of new technology.[10]

Nanotechnology could completely revolutionize medicine and contribute to unprecedented human performance through bone and neural tissue engineering, the artificial growth of

human organs for transplants, gene therapy, and many other medical applications.

Bioartificial Organ Manufacturing Technologies / 3D Bioprinting

Bioartificial organ manufacturing technologies are a series of enabling techniques that can be used to produce human organs based on bionic principles. ...One of the most promising bioartificial organ manufacturing technologies is to use combined multi-nozzle three-dimensional printing techniques to automatically assemble personal cells along with other biomaterials to build exclusive organ substitutes for defective/failed human organs. This is the first time that advanced bioartificial organ manufacturing technologies have been reviewed. These technologies hold the promise to greatly improve the quality of health and average lifespan of human beings in the near future.[11]

Artificial Human Eggs, Sperm, and Embryos

Katsuhiko Hayashi, a developmental geneticist at Osaka University, is a pioneer in a highly controversial field of biomedical research—in vitro gametogenesis (IVG).

The goal of IVG is to make unlimited supplies of what Hayashi calls "artificial" eggs and sperm from any cell

in the human body. That could let anyone—older, infertile, single, gay, trans—have their own genetically related babies. Besides the technical challenges that remain to be overcome, there are deep ethical concerns about how IVG might eventually be used.

Conception, a U.S. biotech company, is also racing with Japanese scientists to develop artificial embryos.

IVG would render the biological clock irrelevant, by enabling women of any age to have genetically related children. That raises questions about whether there should be age limits for IVG baby-making. IVG could also enable gay and trans couples to have babies genetically related to both partners, for the first time allowing families, regardless of gender identity, to have biologically related children.

Beyond that, IVG could potentially make traditional baby-making antiquated for everyone. An unlimited supply of genetically matched artificial human eggs, sperm and embryos for anyone, anytime could make scanning the genes of IVG embryos the norm. Prospective parents would be able to minimize the chances their children would be born with detrimental genes. IVG could also lead to "designer babies," whose parents pick and choose the traits they desire.[12]

Designer Babies

Emerging technologies may soon allow parents to select specific traits for their children, such as strength, intelligence, eye color, etc. This would also likely create vast disparities in genetic strengths based on socioeconomic status.

Other Emerging Technologies

The list of such technologies could go on at length. Some researchers are developing synthetic human blood. Others are working on cloaking devices. Many are discussing various implants. A robotic exoskeleton was recently developed to help runners sprint faster. Cyborg technology continues to advance, as does stem cell therapy. Various members of the super wealthy class are "bio-hacking" their way to becoming "younger" and extending their lifespans. Then there's the notion of the metaverse—and what it might mean for humans to exist as avatars in a virtual world or to share consciousness in a "hive mind." Clearly, we are stepping into some new frontiers.

Artificial Intelligence

On a somewhat separate (but related) note, artificial intelligence (AI) is now making headlines on a daily basis, and the new technology is already disrupting many industries. It's changing how we think and operate in virtually every major field. The advent of AI has caused a deluge of questions from legislators, regulators, ethicists, businessmen, and even the AI developers themselves. No one seems to really know where this

might lead, and some even fear eventual human extinction in one form or another as AI becomes more pervasive and more powerful. Unfortunately, however, the evolution and spread of AI is far outpacing our ability to understand and regulate it.

SPIRIT-LED OR AI-DEPENDENT?

At the height of its power, the British Empire ruled over a quarter of the world. As the foremost global power, they would appoint governors over their various colonies to acclimate these new territories to British ways, with the intent of making the colonies reflect the culture of their colonizers. (The term *colonization* is derived from the Latin word *colere,* which means to cultivate a land as a farmer.) It is for this reason that many African nations, and many other nations around the world, not only speak their native language but also the language of their colonizers.

Analogous to this, though with vastly different tactics, the Holy Spirit was sent to the earth as the Governor of the Church to ensure that the people of God are cultivated in the ways of the heavenly Kingdom, for the Church is meant to be a territory or colony of heaven in the earth. And just as British colonizers influenced the languages and cultures of their colonies, the Holy Spirit's role is to guide believers into the culture of the Kingdom of God. As the apostle Paul writes, *"our citizenship is in heaven, and from it we await a Savior, the Lord Jesus Christ"* (Philippians 3:20, ESV). As believers, we are truly citizens of the heavenly Kingdom right now, with all of its associated rights and privileges.

Again, the Holy Spirit's role as Governor is to ensure our complete acclimation into the Kingdom Society. He is responsible for guiding us into all truth, showing us things to come, teaching us all things, helping us pray according to the will of God, empowering us with supernatural gifts, mantling us to serve in Kingdom positions and offices, sanctifying us, and providing comfort. In the same way that the disciples were totally dependent upon the physical presence of Jesus, the Church must now be totally dependent upon the Spirit of Jesus, which is the Holy Spirit.

Consider a few of the words of Jesus on the role of the Holy Spirit in the life of the Church:

> And I will pray the Father, and he shall give you another Comforter, that he may abide with you for ever; even the Spirit of truth; whom the world cannot receive, because it seeth him not, neither knoweth him: but ye know him; for he dwelleth with you, and shall be in you. I will not leave you comfortless: I will come to you (**John 14:16-18, KJV**).

> These things have I spoken unto you, being yet present with you. But the Comforter, which is the Holy Ghost, whom the Father will send in my name, he shall teach you all things, and bring all things to your remembrance, whatsoever I have said unto you (**John 14:25-26, KJV**).

> I have yet many things to say unto you, but ye cannot bear them now. Howbeit when he, the Spirit of truth, is come, he will guide you into all truth: for he shall not speak of himself; but whatsoever he shall hear,

that shall he speak: and he will shew you things to come. He shall glorify me: for he shall receive of mine, and shall shew it unto you. All things that the Father hath are mine: therefore said I, that he shall take of mine, and shall shew it unto you (**John 16:12-15; KJV**).

Over the years, I have discovered the importance of becoming a student of the Holy Spirit. I have learned that He can be quenched and grieved by actions that dishonor Christ or disregard His presence. There have been instances when the Holy Spirit woke me between 3:00 and 4:00 in the morning, imparting insights about Christ and His Kingdom. I would absorb these teachings until my spirit was full, then write and study the revelations. His guidance comes through subtle promptings, explicit directives, and visions and dreams. I recall one moment when the Holy Spirit stirred me to pray for a relative, and He was making intercession through me for the safety of this person. I prayed with Him until the burden lifted, and later that day I discovered that she had narrowly avoided a fatal car accident at the very hour I was prompted to pray. The Lord spared her from potential tragedy.

To foster an intimate relationship with the Holy Spirit, it is necessary to dedicate time in daily prayer to listen to Him with your heart. I am confident that those who learn to hear Him in private will also have an ear for Him in public spaces. Can you imagine an entire community of believers being collectively guided by the Holy Spirit into all of His divine realities? What would be possible if all believers were empowered by the Holy Spirit to authentically reveal Jesus to the world? What would it be like if the Church functioned like a heavenly colony in the

earth? I believe this part of God's dream will be revealed in our day. We will be that city on a hill that is impossible to conceal.

Such a reality thrives where there is spiritual maturity. "*For as many as are led by the Spirit of God, they are the sons of God*" (Romans 8:14, KJV). The word *sons* in its original language refers to mature sons. God is maturing believers today to be genuinely led by the Holy Spirit in every aspect of life. This is the Church founded on the rock of Christ Jesus, against which the gates of hell will not prevail.

However, my concern today is how AI-dependency could begin to infringe on the spaces that belong to the Holy Spirit. There could come a time, and it might be here already, when ministers seek ChatGPT for sermon inspiration before devoting time to prayer. Instead of waiting on the Holy Spirit for a word of wisdom or a word of knowledge, believers may turn to the counsel of AI. What if the Holy Spirit wanted to inspire someone to record a new song, write a script for a movie, create a heavenly reality in the earth, or heal a memory, but escaping reality through the metaverse (or some other manufactured reality) was easier?

I believe that AI and other forms of technology are intended to support human wellness—not replace our need for truth with an elaborate lie. We are entering a period in which escapism may be utilized regularly in an attempt to stabilize the mental health of people. As opposed to working out in the gym, maintaining a healthy diet, and living a healthy lifestyle, it may be easier to electronically modify our photos and use available technologies to alter our external appearance. Once again, technology itself is neither good nor evil, but we must be conscious about how it is being used and what level of dependency it is creating.

Is it possible for a generation to grow so dependent upon AI that we forget the Holy Spirit's work of guiding us into all truth? Is it possible that we will forfeit our own creative ability by deferring to AI to think and create for us? God has mandated that humans rule the earth in His stead, and that includes subduing technology so that it becomes a tool but never the rule. I really believe that AI can enhance what we do, as long as it remains subordinate to the Holy Spirit, but striking that balance is crucial. We must ensure that our use of AI does not overshadow our connection with the Holy Spirit or stifle our God-given creative potential. The authentically Spirit-led generation will harness technology for Kingdom advancement without losing sight of its intended purpose.

THE IMAGE OF GOD: GOD'S PLAN FOR HUMAN ENHANCEMENT

God's plan for human enhancement, standing in stark contrast to the path of transhumanism, involves "putting on" Christ and being transformed into God's image in the earth. This involves receiving supernatural character traits, authorities, and powers that are beyond "normal" human capacity. The rest of this book will focus on training the believer to "put on" Christ for higher human functionality. First, however, we must ground our discussion in God's original design for humanity; we must learn the human blueprint.

NOTES

1. *Oxford Languages*, s.v. "transhumanism."

2. René Ostberg, "transhumanism," *Encyclopedia Britannica*, August 29, 2023, https://www.britannica.com/topic/transhumanism.

3. Ibid.

4. "Lord Shiva Statue Unveiled." *CERN Document Server*, July 5, 2004, https://cds.cern.ch/record/745737?ln=en.

5. "What are genome editing and CRISPR-Cas9?" *MedlinePlus [Internet], Bethesda (MD): National Library of Medicine (US)*, March 22, 2022, https://medlineplus.gov/genetics/understanding/genomicresearch/genomeediting.

6. "CRISPR," *National Human Genome Research Institute*, January 24, 2024, www.genome.gov/genetics-glossary/CRISPR.

7. Kara Rogers, "gene doping," *Encyclopedia Britannica,* August 17, 2023, https://www.britannica.com/science/gene-doping.

8. *Neuralink*, https://neuralink.com, accessed January 31, 2024.

9. "About Cryonics," *The Cryonics Institute*, https://cryonics.org/about-cryonics, accessed January 31, 2024.

10. "Nanotechnology," *Centers for Disease Control and Prevention*, September 8, 2023, www.cdc.gov/niosh/topics/nanotech/default.html.

11. Wang X, "Bioartificial Organ Manufacturing Technologies," *Cell Transplant,* January 2019, 28(1):5-17, doi: 10.1177/0963689718809918.

12. Rob Stein, "Japanese scientists race to create human eggs and sperm in the lab," *NPR*, September 28, 2023.

CHAPTER 3

THE HUMAN
BLUEPRINT

MY TESTIMONY: DELIVERED FROM
THE SPIRIT OF DEATH

During my childhood, I was plagued by many existential questions, along with many difficult-to-explain spiritual experiences. This built within me an insatiable appetite to understand the origins of life, death, and the human being. I recall many days and nights sitting on my bed, contemplating these huge subjects and attempting to figure them out. As a nine- or ten-year-old boy, I would get a headache trying to imagine what was before all things. This was my private preoccupation, and it almost destroyed me.

I believe that this could have led to my early demise because I was more preoccupied with death than life. Over the course of much of my early life, I had recurring experiences with what I now identify as the spirit of death. I would be tormented with this agonizing entity many nights while asleep. Later, it began to be accompanied by what I now identify as dream paralysis, and I would be unable to speak or move throughout the night. These horrific experiences built within me a fear of death and

an even greater preoccupation with it. I vividly remember dreaming of my own demise in the city where I was born and raised. Driving through the city, I would often see that place and say to myself, "One day I may lose my life there."

My childhood was laced with fainting, seizures, and the medically unexplained, which culminated in a life-threatening heart attack at the tender age of 18. This took place when I arrived home after my first semester of college. I had a fainting episode, and I was told by a doctor that I had experienced an attack. The medical staff also expressed nervousness about the possibility of triggering an additional attack. They would not permit me to engage in any physical activity while in the hospital for eight days.

After I was released from the hospital, my mother, Georgia L. Howard, invited me to Bethlehem Temple, a small Pentecostal church in the city of my origin. I listened to the minister, and to this day I recall only one statement from his message. I remember him emphatically declaring to the audience, "You do not have to be a slave of sin!" It felt like God was talking directly to me in that moment. It was as if the heavens opened and I saw the holiness of God. I began crying like a baby, which was completely outside of my character as an 18-year-old college basketball jock.

That very day, I was baptized in the name of the Lord Jesus Christ, and I was filled with the Holy Spirit, with the evidence of speaking in tongues. And it was at my next doctor's appointment that I learned that my heart condition was healed! The doctors could not find anything in my current condition that matched what they had originally diagnosed. I now know that God not only saved my soul, but He healed my body in the same day.

This experience prompted me to pursue God with my heart. I desperately wanted to know this God and understand His redemptive work for humanity. I now know that God delivered me from the spirit of death that was dominating my human spirit, influencing my soul, and attempting to kill my body. After nearly 40 years of study and insights from the Holy Spirit, I now have a measure of clarity regarding what I experienced and how the redemptive work of Christ Jesus can enhance and deliver the human spirit, restore the human soul, and heal the human body. In this chapter, I will explain in detail the anatomy of the triune human being.

THE PERFECT HUMAN

When God was giving Moses instructions for the construction of the Tabernacle, He said, *"You must build this Tabernacle and its furnishings exactly according to the pattern I will show you"* (Exodus 25:9, NLT). God gave Moses a heavenly pattern, and Moses was commanded to build the earthly Tabernacle exactly according to the pattern that God showed him in the heavens. When he completed this task, God's glory filled the house in an incredible way.

In fact, if any architect or builder engages in any significant work of construction, they must frequently consult the blueprint. They must reference the original design and build according to the pattern so that the final product will be an accurate reflection of that original design.

The same is true for us as human beings. If we are to understand who we are, we must look at the blueprint. We know that

we were originally made in the image of God and after His likeness, but that image was marred by sin. Thankfully, Christ came as *"the image of the invisible God"* (Colossians 1:15, NIV) to restore that image in humanity. Christ, then, is our perfect Human Blueprint. He is the Second Man, the Last Adam. He is the pattern according to which we now build. The psalmist encourages us to *"mark the perfect man, and behold the upright: for the end of that man is peace"* (Psalm 37:37, KJV).

In later sections of this book, we will discover how to "put on" Christ and become an enhanced human being; but first, we must understand our own human anatomy—how we have been constructed by God—so that we can properly appropriate the enhancement that Christ is offering.

THE TRICHOTOMOUS HUMAN TEMPLE

In the Old Testament, the Temple (and earlier, the Tabernacle) was a place of worship that consisted of three main sections: the Outer Court, the Inner Court, and the Most Holy Place. God filled the Temple with His glory, and the Temple became a place of overlap between heaven and earth.

In the New Testament, we discover that the physical Temple, while significant, was only a type and shadow of the real temple: the human being. The apostle Paul writes, *"Don't you know that you yourselves are God's temple and that God's Spirit dwells in your midst?"* (1 Corinthians 3:16, NIV). God desires for us as human beings to be filled with His glory and to become the living portals between heaven and earth.

In fact, the Old Testament Temple represents Christ, the perfect human being, and the spiritual temple in heaven. Like this Temple, we as human beings are made up of three main parts: spirit, soul, and body. More precisely, we are spirits, we possess souls, and we live in bodies. Paul again writes, *"May God himself, the God of peace, sanctify you through and through May your whole spirit, soul and body be kept blameless at the coming of our Lord Jesus Christ"* (1 Thessalonians 5:23, NIV). God was very particular about how He wanted the Old Testament Temple constructed, in part because it represented the human being. The human body is represented by the Outer Court, the human soul is represented by the Inner Court, and the human spirit is represented by the Most Holy Place.

It is also fascinating that all three of these parts—spirit, soul, and body—are present in the description of the creation of humanity:

> *And the Lord God formed man of the **dust of the ground** [body], and breathed into his nostrils the **breath of life** [spirit]; and man became a **living soul*** (**Genesis 2:7, KJV**).

If we are going to learn how to "put on" Christ and become enhanced humans, we must first understand our own design— spirit, soul, and body. Our spirits make us God-conscious, our souls make us self-conscious, and our bodies make us world-conscious. Put another way, our spirits allow us to perceive the spirit world, our souls allow us to perceive the inner world, and our bodies allow us to perceive the physical world. The divine enhancement of a human being involves awakening

Christ in the human spirit, forming Christ in the human soul, and expressing Christ through the human body.

These three main parts of us—spirit, soul, and body—are also incredibly interrelated and interconnected. Though we discuss them separately for the sake of making helpful distinctions, there is constant interaction between them. And though it can, at times, be challenging to know what is happening within us, the writer of Hebrews assures us that *"the word of God is alive and active. Sharper than any double-edged sword, it penetrates even to dividing soul and spirit, joints and marrow; it judges the thoughts and attitudes of the heart"* (Hebrews 4:12, NIV).

Once again, in his first epistle to the Thessalonians, the apostle Paul prays for the God of peace to wholly sanctify his readers: *"And the very God of peace sanctify you wholly; and I pray God your whole spirit and soul and body be preserved blameless unto the coming of our Lord Jesus Christ"* (1 Thessalonians 5:23, KJV). The word *wholly* in this verse means to be uniquely and entirely set apart according to the divine design. The inference is that every part of the human being was created to reveal God in some capacity.

Imagine a mother directing her children to clean their bedroom wholly or completely. This, of course, means more than just making the bed. The mother's expectation would be for her children to clean the closet, the drawers, under the bed, the nightstand, the floor, and every other part of the room. My mother believes a good housecleaning requires everything to be put in its rightful place. Her mantra is "everything has a place." Analogous to this, Paul's hope was that the whole spirit, soul, and body of the Thessalonians would be set apart and yielded to God, which is the end of the sanctification process.

Paul's description of the human constitution helps us to accurately envision the full essence of a human life-form. The human being is like a house with many levels, rooms, and furnishings. Each aspect of our person is meant to be fully operative, functioning according to the divine design. The fulfillment of Paul's prayer for total sanctification would position the Thessalonians to shine as bright lights illuminating the path for many travelers.

Perhaps this is why the psalmist writes, *"I will praise thee; for I am fearfully and wonderfully made: marvellous are thy works; and that my soul knoweth right well"* (Psalm 139:14, KJV). Another version of this verse says, *"I will give thanks to you because I have been so amazingly and miraculously made. Your works are miraculous, and my soul is fully aware of this"* (GW). Still another says, *"Thank you for making me so wonderfully complex! Your workmanship is marvelous—how well I know it"* (NLT).

These statements insist that humanity was made with an awe-inspiring splendor and a uniqueness that contains intrinsic value and attraction. I am absolutely persuaded that everyone who is trained in the proper use of their whole spirit, soul, and body will discover a life of unlimited possibilities. The truth of our brilliant creation is intended to shatter every lie that seeks to devalue or imprison people in alternate realities or some inhumane state of existence.

Let us now examine each of these three components of the human construct: the human spirit, the human soul, and the human body.

THE HUMAN SPIRIT

In the Old Testament, the Hebrew word *ruach* is translated "spirit" in our English Bibles. It can also be translated as "breath" or "wind." In the New Testament, the Greek word *pneuma* is used, and the definitions are essentially the same.

The human spirit is the essence of a person—the core of their personhood. It can be likened to breath or wind. It can also be likened to a burning fire, as one of the stars in the night sky. It is the "throne" that a person occupies in the spirit world—the fullness of their heavenly identity. In the Old Testament Temple, it is typified by the Most Holy Place, the sacred space that held the Ark of the Covenant—upon which was the mercy seat of God Himself.

Our Creator has fashioned us much like Himself. God is Spirit and Light, and therefore, humans are spirit-beings and light-beings. Our spirits allow us to be conscious of God and the spirit world, and we have the capacity to use our spiritual senses to see, taste, touch, smell, and hear in that realm. Spiritual sight grants us the ability to experience spiritual visions and dreams. Spiritual taste signifies a transformative encounter; true taste emerges when we are fully immersed in something. Spiritual touch occurs when we are profoundly affected by another person's condition or action. Spiritual smell involves discerning differences in spiritual matters. Spiritual hearing is the capacity to perceive the voice of God.

In fact, there are all kinds of activities that can take place in the spirit world. It is possible to learn how to travel in the spirit, communicate in the spirit, war in the spirit, receive in

the spirit, and so much more. It is imperative that we as believers learn how to fully operate in this spiritual space.

The Holy Spirit is the one who guides us into all truth, and He is the one who guides all our activity in the spirit world. Our spirit consciousness allows us to perceive the Holy Spirit, to pray in the Spirit, to activate our spiritual instincts, to perceive angelic and demonic spirits, to receive spiritual gifts, to understand spiritual callings, to put on spiritual garments, to receive God-given visions and dreams, and to praise and worship with spiritual songs.

As born-again believers, our spirits have been seated with Christ *"in the heavenly places in Christ Jesus"* (Ephesians 2:6, ESV), and there are many places in the heavenly realms that we may (by the Spirit) be given access to:

- The Third Heaven

- The Throne of Grace

- The Heavenly Council

- The Courts of Heaven

- The Hosts of Heaven

- The Bank of Heaven

- Spiritual territories

- Spiritual communities

- The spiritual dimensions associated with the death, burial, resurrection, ascension, and rule of Jesus Christ

- …and much more!

The apostle Paul writes that "*all who are led by the Spirit of God are sons of God*" (Romans 8:14, ESV). We must be Spirit-led in all that we think, say, and do. The human spirit is a covering for the human soul, just as the human soul is a covering for the human body; and very often, our spirits perceive and know things that our conscious minds do not yet comprehend. Therefore, we must learn how to submit the conscious mind to the Spirit of God and adopt His positions on every matter.

Paul makes it clear that we can only search the deep things of God by the Spirit of God:

> *However, as it is written: "What no eye has seen, what no ear has heard, and what no human mind has conceived"—the things God has prepared for those who love him—these are the things God has revealed to us by his Spirit. The Spirit searches all things, even the deep things of God. For who knows a person's thoughts except their own spirit within them? In the same way no one knows the thoughts of God except the Spirit of God. What we have received is not the spirit of the world, but the Spirit who is from God, so that we may understand what God has freely given us. This is what we speak, not in words taught us by human wisdom but in words taught by the Spirit, explaining spiritual realities with Spirit-taught words. The person without the Spirit does not accept the things that come from the Spirit of God but considers them foolishness, and cannot understand them because they are discerned only through the Spirit. The person with the Spirit makes judgments about all things, but such a person is not subject to merely*

human judgments, for, "Who has known the mind of the Lord so as to instruct him?" But we have the mind of Christ (**1 Corinthians 2:9-16, NIV**).

Remember, God says, "*As the heavens are higher than the earth, so are my ways higher than your ways and my thoughts than your thoughts*" (Isaiah 55:9, NIV). And Jesus said, "*God is spirit, and those who worship him must worship in spirit and truth*" (John 4:24, ESV). That means that God primarily communicates with us through our spirits. We must allow our spirits to be led by the Holy Spirit, and we must train our souls and bodies to align and follow.

We must also learn to "take inventory" of what is in our spirits at any given time—to understand our spiritual "anatomy." Our human spirits will be filled either with the genuine fruit of Christ's Spirit or some distorted version of it. We will either activate the new nature of Christ in our human spirits or succumb to the old Adamic nature. For example:

Christ's Spirit	Spiritual Distortions
Love	Fear, Hate, Lust, Anger
Joy	Defeat, Weakness, Agony, Depression
Peace	Discord, Lack, Brokenness, Restlessness, Anxiety
Patience	Mercilessness, Impatience, Irritability, Lack of Endurance
Kindness	Rudeness, Thoughtlessness, Carelessness

Christ's Spirit	Spiritual Distortions
Goodness	Commonness, Mediocrity, Dysfunction
Faithfulness	Unreliability, Disloyalty, Irresponsibility, Falsehood
Gentleness / Meekness	Disobedience, Immodesty, Arrogance
Self-Mastery	Over-Indulgence, Lack of Discipline, Addiction
Wisdom	Foolishness, Silliness, Lack of Perception, Lack of Distinction
Truth	Deception, Dishonesty, Illusion
Benevolence	Stinginess, Selfishness, Greed, Hoarding
Justice	Injustice, Inequity, Imbalance, Unfairness
Zeal	Selfish Ambition
Power	Powerlessness, Victimhood, Deceleration, Weakness

The essence, condition, and health of the human spirit are determined by the entity with which it communes. The human spirit consumes and assumes the substance of whatever spirit it is in constant contact with. We were designed to worship, so it is natural for the human spirit to become whatever it focuses on or has intimate fellowship with. For example, the human

spirit will become fear if it is in fellowship with fear. It will activate the old nature and become deceitful if it is in constant fellowship with a lying spirit. Alternatively, the human spirit will activate the new nature, become love, and send loving thoughts to the conscious mind if it is in constant contact with the Spirit of a loving God.

With this in mind, *"let us cleanse ourselves from all filthiness of the flesh and spirit, perfecting holiness in the fear of God"* (2 Corinthians 7:1, KJV). Lord, make us aware of our spirit's preoccupation and communion, and allow Christ to awaken inside of our spirits!

THE HUMAN SOUL

In addition to our spirit, we have an intangible soul with many parts that together allow for self-consciousness, self-determination, and an entire inner world that enables us to function like a human bank, holding in trust heavenly treasures.

The human soul, as a place of worship, is typified by the Inner Court of the Temple. The Inner Court contained three important features: the Altar of Incense, the Table of Showbread, and the Candlestick. All three of these features must be present in a healthy human soul:

- Altar of Incense: Prayer, praise, and worship that ascends to God

- Table of Showbread: The daily "rhema" Word of God

- The Candlestick: The anointing oil and illumination of the Holy Spirit

The human soul has at least nine major, identifiable parts:

1. Will
2. Intellect
3. Imagination
4. Emotion
5. Conscience
6. Codes
7. Memories
8. Values
9. Belief Systems

We will briefly describe each of these nine components.

Will

The human will is the expression of self-determination. This part of the soul is responsible for making decisions, following resolute plans, and "cutting" certain realities in order to shape the future.

There are at least four types of wills:

1. Strong Will (diligence)
2. Stubborn Will (rebellion and witchcraft)
3. Weak Will (vulnerability and inconsistency)
4. Broken Will (incontinence)

The human will acts like an architectural design of a city—determining what reality will be constructed within the life of the person. Therefore, the will must be surrendered and combined with the will of God for maximum benefit and power. Like Jesus, we must pray, "*not my will, but yours be done*" (Luke 22:42, NIV). Believers must ultimately do the will of God, and we are encouraged by the fact that it is He who works in us "*both to will and to do of his good pleasure*" (Philippians 2:13, KJV).

Intellect

The human intellect is "the faculty of reasoning and understanding objectively, especially with regard to abstract or academic matters."[1] Intellectual reasoning consists of thoughts and trains of thoughts. A thought is "an idea or opinion produced by thinking, or occurring suddenly in the mind."[2]

The purpose of the human intellect is to create purpose and influence the human will. Individual thoughts act like seeds that can germinate and produce more thoughts.

Imagination

The human imagination is "the faculty or action of forming new ideas, or images or concepts of external objects not present to the senses."[3] It can also be defined as "the act or power of forming a mental image of something not present to the senses or never before wholly perceived in reality."[4] Essentially, the imagination is the "image creation" center of the soul, and its

purpose is to provide visuals of what is possible and to generate supportive intellectual arguments.

Albert Einstein famously said, "Imagination is more important than knowledge. For knowledge is limited, whereas imagination embraces the entire world, stimulating progress, giving birth to evolution."[5]

Emotion

Emotion is "a natural instinctive state of mind deriving from one's circumstances, mood, or relationships with others."[6] It can also be defined as an "instinctive or intuitive feeling as distinguished from reasoning or knowledge"[7] or "a conscious mental reaction (such as anger or fear) subjectively experienced as strong feeling usually directed toward a specific object and typically accompanied by physiological and behavioral changes in the body."[8]

The purpose of human emotion is to create atmospheres that move, bless, and connect people. Here are a few examples of common human emotions:

- Anger
- Sadness
- Fear
- Happiness
- Anxiety
- Disgust

- Shame
- Surprise
- Guilt
- Love
- Boredom
- Embarrassment

- Satisfaction
- Envy
- Depression
- Loneliness
- Jealousy
- Frustration
- Contempt
- Pride
- Disappointment
- Amusement
- Awe

Conscience

The human conscience is "an inner feeling or voice viewed as acting as a guide to the rightness or wrongness of one's behavior."[9] The conscience is essentially the judgment hall of the soul, and its purpose is to provide moral judgments with regard to all personal behavior. The conscience can be in one of at least four different conditions:

1. Strong Conscience: a cleansed conscience that reflects God's judgments

2. Weak Conscience: an overly scrupulous conscience

3. Seared Conscience: a conscience devoid of feeling

4. Broken Conscience: a misinformed conscience

Codes

A *code* is a collection or system of rules of conduct. It can also be defined as "a systematic statement of a body of law, especially

one given statutory force."[10] Human codes deal with the personal philosophies that we have about life and the way we want to live it. These codes determine how we define ourselves, the values we work toward, and the information upon which we base our decisions. They are personal laws that are written within us, and some refer to them as "life commandments."

The purpose of codes is to create a set of instructions for the soul to follow. These instructions determine what actions the soul can and cannot take. In the computing world, coding allows programmers to build programs. In similar fashion, human codes "program" the person to operate a certain way.

Memories

The *memory* is "the faculty by which the mind stores and remembers information."[11] Put another way, it is "the term given to the structures and processes involved in the storage and subsequent retrieval of information."[12] There are at least four types of memory: working, sensory, short-term, and long-term.

Essentially, the human memory is the archives of the soul. It is the record-keeper of all of our experiences. Positive memories can be written deep in the heart, and so can traumatic memories. In one case, God said that *"the sin of Judah is written with a pen of iron; with a point of diamond it is engraved on the tablet of their heart, and on the horns of their altars"* (Jeremiah 17:1, ESV). In other words, their sinful experiences had been carved deep into their hearts. Thank God for His power to heal our memories!

Values

Value is defined as "the regard that something is held to deserve; the importance, worth, or usefulness of something."[13] Our values involve our appraisal process, and they determine what we deem something to be worth. The purpose of a value system is to create value-based priorities in all things.

Here are a few examples of personal values:

- Loyalty

- Duty

- Respect

- Selfless service

- Honor

- Integrity

- Personal courage

Belief Systems

Belief is "an acceptance that a statement is true or that something exists" or "trust, faith, or confidence in someone or something."[14] It can also be defined as "a state or habit of mind in which trust or confidence is placed in some person or thing."[15]

The purpose of the belief system is to create accurate mental models and erect the image of Christ in the mind with supporting arguments.

THE HUMAN BODY

Finally, our bodies serve as containers designed to house our incorporeal parts as well as manifest invisible realities in this physical world.

The human body is typified by the Outer Court of the Temple. Just as animal sacrifices were made on the altar in the Outer Court, we are admonished in Scripture to present our bodies as *"a living sacrifice, holy, acceptable unto God"* (Romans 12:1, KJV). The body, made by God from the dust of the ground, consists of several interconnected systems and structures, as well as the five senses that allow us to be conscious of the world around us—hearing, sight, taste, touch, and smell.

The body is intended to enable us to express and manifest Christ on earth in tangible ways, and all of our body parts must be dedicated to Him. The apostle Paul writes, *"Do you not know that your bodies are temples of the Holy Spirit, who is in you, whom you have received from God? You are not your own; you were bought at a price. Therefore honor God with your bodies"* (1 Corinthians 6:19-20, NIV).

Our body parts are intended to be instruments of war in God's hands, and therefore, they must be trained in righteousness. It is Paul again who writes:

> *Do you not know that in a race all the runners run, but only one gets the prize? Run in such a way as to get the prize. Everyone who competes in the games goes into strict training. They do it to get a crown that will not last, but we do it to get a crown that will last forever. Therefore I do not run like someone*

running aimlessly; I do not fight like a boxer beating the air. No, I strike a blow to my body and make it my slave so that after I have preached to others, I myself will not be disqualified for the prize (**1 Corinthians 9:24-27, NIV**).

Healthy, Spirit-inspired routines help us to train our bodies. We must adopt certain regulations and protocols in our lives that will contribute to healthy bodies and bodily self-mastery. Over time, this will create a positive "muscle memory" as our bodies become accustomed to God-honoring disciplines. We must manage our diets, our hydration levels, our exercise routines, our sleep patterns, and our levels of sensory stimulation in all areas.

SPIRIT OVER SOUL, SOUL OVER BODY

Many people feel overwhelmed and stretched thin in their minds and emotions because their human souls have become elevated above their human spirits. The human soul—composed of will, intellect, imagination, emotion, conscience, codes, memories, values, and belief systems—was never meant to take precedence over the human spirit. Just as a husband covers his wife or a father covers his daughters, the human spirit is designed to cover the human soul. Like an uncovered wife, an uncovered daughter, or even an uncovered plate of food, an uncovered human soul is vulnerable to contamination.

In light of this, I encourage you to refrain from reacting emotionally, speaking randomly, acting presumptuously, or

imagining aimlessly. These behaviors typically arise when the soul elevates itself above the spirit. The role of the human spirit is to receive knowledge and power from the Spirit of God, surpassing anything taught at a conscious level. When the human soul is covered by a human spirit filled with the knowledge and power of God, it will be guided in all that is good and right.

Those who experience this level of spiritual growth will not be overwhelmed and stretched thin in their souls. Instead, they will prioritize spirit over soul and soul over body. In doing so, they will find both peace and power in all their endeavors.

A WORD OF ENCOURAGEMENT

As you can see, we as humans are highly complex beings. We are God's masterpieces, intricately woven together for His glory. There are so many parts and facets to us—so many rooms and dimensions within us. In light of this, the greatest knowledge that we can acquire, other than the knowledge of God, is the knowledge of self. We must know ourselves, inside and out, so that we can manifest the purpose of God for our lives.

However, because of our complexity, it can sometimes be difficult to fully understand what is going on within us. It can be challenging to assess our condition and accurately diagnose issues. And each part within us has ripple effects on all the other parts. If one thing is off, it can be like a highly technical computer going haywire, requiring a trained specialist to fix the problem. This level of complexity can be discouraging for some.

Therefore, I would like to offer you some encouragement. When speaking to the rich young ruler, Jesus said, "*You lack one thing*" (Mark 10:21, ESV). After decades of ministry, I have discovered that most people only have one or two major personal challenges to overcome in their lives. The Bible speaks of "*the sin which so easily entangles us*" (Hebrews 12:1, NASB). All of us have a specific weakness to overcome, and this one challenge could be impacting several areas of our spirits, souls, and bodies.

But take heart! This means that once this one issue is properly addressed and overcome, you will experience explosive growth and forward progress. You are not ruined. Your case is not hopeless. You may only have one thing that needs fixing— one thing standing in between you and the greatest triumph of your life. One small adjustment could trigger an unprecedented breakthrough.

I also encourage you to be patient with yourself. It can take time to get to know yourself, so take a deep breath and settle in. This journey of self-discovery is a lifelong pursuit. Despite what you may think, you are not late in your self-discovery process. Just as it took time for Israel to take the Promised Land, so our occupation of the "inner Promised Land" is progressive in nature. You are on the right track, so keep going!

READY FOR ENHANCEMENT

Now that we understand the basic mechanics of the human being, we are ready to dive into God's plan for human enhancement!

NOTES

1. *Oxford Languages*, s.v. "intellect."

2. Ibid., s.v. "thought."

3. Ibid., s.v. "imagination."

4. *Merriam-Webster's Dictionary*, s.v. "imagination," https://www.merriam-webster.com/dictionary/imagination.

5. Albert Einstein, "Einstein on Cosmic Religion and Other Opinions and Aphorisms" (Mineola, New York: Dover Publication, 2009), 97. (This Dover edition is an unabridged republication of *Cosmic Religion and Other Opinions and Aphorisms*, originally published in 1931 by Covici-Friede, Inc., New York.

6. *Oxford Languages*, s.v. "emotion."

7. Ibid.

8. *Merriam-Webster's Dictionary*, s.v. "emotion," https://www.merriam-webster.com/dictionary/emotion.

9. *Oxford Languages*, s.v. "conscience."

10. *Merriam-Webster's Dictionary*, s.v. "code," https://www.merriam-webster.com/dictionary/code.

11. *Oxford Languages*, s.v. "memory."

12. Saul Mcleod, "Memory Stages: Encoding Storage and Retrieval," *SimplyPsychology*, edited by Olivia Guy-Evans, June 16, 2023, www.simplypsychology.org/memory.html.

13. *Oxford Languages*, s.v. "value."

14. Ibid., s.v. "belief."

15. *Merriam-Webster's Dictionary*, s.v. "belief," https://www.merriam-webster.com/dictionary/belief.

CHAPTER 4

GOD'S PLAN FOR HUMAN ENHANCEMENT

SUPERNATURALLY ENHANCED HUMANS

In the New Testament, God's people operated with some incredible supernatural abilities. At the word of Jesus, Peter walked on water. Later, Peter walked by those who were sick on the street, and his shadow healed them of their ailments. In another instance, he spoke a word, and a man and his wife immediately fell dead for lying to the Holy Spirit. Philip vanished and reappeared by the power of the Holy Spirit. Paul struck a man blind for a time.

In fact, all "*the apostles performed many signs and wonders among the people*" (Acts 5:12, NIV). Their prison doors were miraculously opened. They praised God, and earthquakes shook the ground. They spoke in unknown spiritual languages. They cast out demons. They healed the sick. They raised the dead. They accurately predicted future events. They rejoiced in persecution and willingly sacrificed their lives for Christ, confident of the resurrection to come.

If all of these incredible feats were relegated to a bygone time, it might be easy for some to write them off as ancient myths or

fairy tales. But these supernatural abilities are still operative today. In my own life and the lives of others, I have witnessed countless examples of miracles, signs, and wonders. I have seen people healed, demons cast out, and future events foretold. I have experienced visions, dreams, and powerful encounters with God Almighty. I have seen lives radically transformed by the power of God.

On one occasion, following a visit to a heart specialist, I received an unexpected report: my heart had undergone what my doctor deemed its own bypass surgery, marking me as a medical mystery. I attribute this unexplained healing to the supernatural power of God. Through learning to access Christ as a Healer, I have experienced divine intervention in my health for several years—including healing a degenerating disc, averting recommended back surgery, and overcoming conditions like high blood pressure.

In another instance, the Lord guided me to sell a church facility and build a new one, promising a doubling in the size of the congregation if I followed these instructions. Obediently, we sold our church property, temporarily leasing facilities for approximately two years, and we witnessed our ministry double before dedicating our new church edifice—a testament to the miraculous power of God.

Recently, we witnessed God bring healing to a baby who was diagnosed with a fetal intracranial hemorrhage. The married couple was expecting a son, due September 24, 2023. At 20 weeks into the pregnancy, an ultrasound revealed a mildly enlarged ventricle in the brain. On May 2, a follow-up ultrasound showed severe bleeding/blood on the left side of the brain (a level 4 out of 4), mild bleeding/blood on the right side of the brain, as well as a slight malformation of some facial

features. At a follow-up appointment with the University of Michigan on May 10, the same findings were confirmed, along with potential deterioration of some of the brain (given the blood).

The diagnosis was a fetal intracranial hemorrhage (essentially a stroke in the womb). The doctors were unsure what caused this, as the mother was very healthy and had a complication-free pregnancy prior to this one. Given the severity of the bleeding, the doctors expected the child to have severe physical and mental challenges, in the rare event that he survived. Due to this, the doctors advised the couple to abort the child.

Hearing this news, the couple reached out to us for support. Following prayer, the Lord directed us not to terminate the pregnancy but instead to prophesy into the situation, make divine declarations, rebuke the evil one, and release gifts of healing. Our local assembly has multiple Kingdom Order of Ascension Gifts (KOAG) teams trained in redemptive justice practice and dedicated to redemptive casework, and one of our KOAG teams (along with myself) diligently worked on this case until its completion. Ultimately, the baby was born without any complications, demonstrating the healing power of God at work.

Throughout my journey, the Lord has brought physical healing, inner healing, and deliverance to many, along with family healing. Additionally, prophetic insights have revealed the future, guiding me in unpopular yet divinely inspired actions. Despite initial challenges, these commands showcased the foresight, brilliance, and power of God as the outcomes unfolded.

The complexities and challenges of our day are putting an intense demand on the people of God to authentically manifest His power like never before. The world is headed into some uncharted territory, and we must fully embrace supernatural enhancement in Christ if we are to effectively represent God and testify to our generation. I hope your appetite is heightened for this kind of enhancement. This chapter is designed to help you experience it for yourself. It all starts with identifying with Christ and experiencing authentic spiritual growth.

AUTHENTIC SPIRITUAL GROWTH

God's plan was always to rule the earth through His image. Humanity was originally made in the image of God and after His likeness, but after the Fall in the Garden, that image was marred. Thankfully, the eternal Word became flesh, and Christ Himself was manifested as *"the image of the invisible God"* to restore that image in the earth (Colossians 1:15, NIV). In light of this, authentic spiritual growth is the process by which the spiritual life is developed into the image of Christ—the perfect human blueprint. From God's vantage point, becoming an enhanced human being involves experiencing personal evolution in Christ.

Once again, the more we see Christ, the more we are transformed into His image and the more power we have to embrace our enhanced humanity. For as we behold Him, we are being *"transformed into the same image from one degree of glory to another"* (2 Corinthians 3:18, ESV), and *"in him we live, and move, and have our being"* (Acts 17:28, KJV).

The process of spiritual growth starts with conception—the new birth experience. When we place our faith in Christ and receive His Holy Spirit, we are "born again," and we become recipients of the divine nature (see 2 Peter 1:2-4). We are born from above with divine DNA, and the "new nature" of Christ is activated within us. Then, with proper care, we eventually grow and develop into a state of full maturation in Christ.

Some of the byproducts of authentic spiritual growth include the following:

- Discovering one's true self

- Ascertaining one's reason for being

- Bringing one's God-ordained purpose to pass

Spiritual growth is as natural as physical growth, and at the most fundamental level, it involves some basic, intuitive practices. Just as our physical bodies thrive based on the quality of our diet, exercise, rest, and overall health, our spirits thrive based on corresponding components:

- Spiritual diet

- Spiritual exercise

- Spiritual rest

- Spiritual health

We must consider each of these factors if we are to become the enhanced humanity in Christ that God is envisioning. What are we consuming spiritually? How are we exercising our spirits and putting our faith into practice? Are we spending

enough time resting our spirits in Christ? What is the overall condition of our spirits?

The journey of spiritual growth in Christ is experienced in seven stages:

1	Lust + Fear	We are manifesting Adam and confused identity.
2	Dependence	We are being nourished by the Church.
3	Independence	We are discovering our gifts and purpose.
4	Interdependence	We are experiencing cooperative ministry within the Body of Christ.
5	Truth + Love	We are manifesting Christ and our true identity.
6	Happiness / Joy	We are experiencing the fullness of the blessing of God.
7	Translation	We are becoming pure light in Him.

THE ART OF BECOMING

This entire journey is about becoming who we were always designed and destined to be in Christ. As believers, we are all being conformed to the image of God, but each of us expresses a unique aspect of that image. If we want to become authentic, spiritually enhanced human beings, then we must actively become who we really are in Christ—with all of the associated character traits, gifts, powers, and benefits.

As the apostle Paul makes clear, we must renounce the "old man" or the old Adamic nature, and we must identify with the

"new man" or the new nature in Christ. If we want to effectively exercise our enhanced abilities in Christ, we must completely consolidate into an entirely new persona. Paul, after speaking of those who still walk in the futility of their old human minds, says the following:

> But you have not so learned Christ, if indeed you have heard Him and have been taught by Him, as the truth is in Jesus: that you put off, concerning your former conduct, the old man which grows corrupt according to the deceitful lusts, and be renewed in the spirit of your mind, and that you put on the new man which was created according to God, in true righteousness and holiness (**Ephesians 4:20-24, NKJV**).

How do we put this into practice? We must personally identify with the death, burial, resurrection, ascension, and reign of Christ Jesus—what I call the Five Laws of the Cross. It was for this reason that Paul said, "*I have been crucified with Christ. It is no longer I who live, but Christ who lives in me. And the life I now live in the flesh I live by faith in the Son of God, who loved me and gave himself for me*" (Galatians 2:20, ESV).

> [The Five Laws of the Cross] are not simply tenants of doctrine that we intellectually ascribe to, nor are they simply historical events that we reflect back upon. They are eternal, living, spiritual laws, and as such, they have the capacity to govern our reality and our lived experience. These spiritual laws are present realities—spiritual dimensions that we can enter into and experience here and now. Only in this way will

we be conformed to Christ, and only in this way will we receive the power to co-rule with Him.

For example, it is not enough simply to intellectually affirm our belief in the death of Christ on the cross. This is good, but it does little by way of transformation. If we want to be transformed by the death of Christ, then we must experience the death of Christ in real-time, as if it were really (spiritually) happening to us in the present moment. We must use our faith to identify with the crucified Christ such that His experience becomes our experience. We must become one with the death of Christ. When this happens, the death of Christ, as a spiritual law, will begin to operate within us, freeing us from the sin nature and everything else that is harming us; and we will reap the tangible benefits of Christ's sacrifice in our real lives.[1]

The apostle Paul declared, *"I die daily"* (1 Corinthians 15:31, KJV)—emphasizing a continuous and present experience. However, it's not merely about daily dying in Christ; it's also about being buried, resurrected, ascended, and reigning each day. Those who make this a daily practice will encounter the transformative power of His death, the purifying effect of His burial, the vitality of His resurrection, the manifestation of His gifts and mantles, and the governing power of royalty to reign in life each day.

I also want to clarify that we do not achieve this solely through human efforts, akin to a doctrine of religious works. On the contrary—it's a profound work of grace. Consider this analogy: just as a laptop can be given WiFi access by the hotspot on a cell phone, all our efforts are fueled by the finished work of

Christ—His death, burial, resurrection, ascension, and reign. Though it might seem like the laptop is functioning independently, it is actually deriving its ability from the hotspot that is energizing it. Similarly, all our endeavors to experience redemption are entirely powered by the living Christ.

Here are the five laws in a nutshell:

The Death of Christ	When we identify with His death, it destroys the sin within us, freeing us from the carnal nature, the demonic kingdom, and the spirit of the world.
The Burial of Christ	When we identify with His burial, we are purged, purified, and cleansed from all unrighteousness. We are separated from all sin, bondage, and corruption, and all negative effects are expunged.
The Resurrection of Christ	When we identify with His resurrection, we are born again, and we receive His new life within us, making us partakers of the divine nature. We triumph over death, hell, and the grave.
The Ascension of Christ	When we identify with His ascension, we experience unconditional acceptance by the Father, and we gain access to spiritual gifts and mantles.
The Reign of Christ	When we identify with His reign, we are given divine authority, and we are empowered to co-rule with Christ as His ambassadors in the earth.

We experience these five laws by believing them, receiving them, meditating on them, vicariously experiencing them, and expressing them in the earth. Collectively, they are the gateway into enhanced humanity.

"PUTTING OFF" THE OLD MAN

Our first step is to "put off the old man"—the old Adamic nature. We were all born with this fallen human nature at work within us, but by experiencing the death and burial of Christ, we can be liberated from it. When we are "crucified with Christ," we allow His death and burial to destroy the old nature that was once alive within us.

It is important to note that the old man cannot be reformed. *"The mind governed by the flesh is hostile to God; it does not submit to God's law, nor can it do so"* (Romans 8:7, NIV). "Self-help" techniques and behavior modification efforts may have some effect on our lives, but ultimately, they are woefully insufficient. We cannot only repent from certain actions. We must become an entirely different person with a completely different (divine) programming. We must renounce the old person and become the new person in Christ Jesus!

To "put off" the old man means to take it off and rend it as one would a garment. The spirit, soul, and body must be completely unclothed from this old nature. At the spirit level, we must renounce our communion with any spirits that are contrary to the Holy Spirit. At the soul level, we must allow the death and burial of Christ to free us, heal us, and cleanse us from all unrighteousness. At the body level, we must separate

ourselves from any unhealthy practices and behaviors that defile the temple of God.

This journey may involve several important practices:

- Daily dying to the old nature

- Receiving inner healing

- Experiencing deliverance from demonic power

- Breaking generational curses

- Renouncing the spirit of the world

(Each of these subjects is a field of study on its own, and we do not have space here to elaborate on each of them, but there are many existing resources in the Kingdom that can assist us in this regard.)

"PUTTING ON" CHRIST FOR HIGHER FUNCTIONALITY

As believers, we are then empowered to *"put on Christ"* (Galatians 3:27, KJV). Put another way, we are empowered to *"put on the new self, which is being renewed in knowledge after the image of its creator"* (Colossians 3:10, ESV). We have ripped apart the old garment; now we are invited to sink into the new garment and clothe ourselves in Christ.

The role of the Holy Spirit in this process is to reveal Christ to our spirits, to guide us into all truth, and to empower us with all the enhancements that we need in Him. Therefore, we must

actively cultivate a relationship with the Holy Spirit. We must watch for His movement, we must host His presence, and we must follow His lead.

When we personally, actively, and consistently experience Christ in His resurrection, ascension, and reign, we gain access to at least three categories of supernatural enhancement:

1. Character

2. Gifts

3. Mantles

Character

First and foremost, when we experience the power of the resurrection of Christ, we become partakers of divine life. The new nature from Christ rises within us, and by His Spirit, we begin to express His character. We could also say that we begin to operate in His name. It is in the name of Jesus that demons are cast out, sicknesses and diseases are healed, and the will of God is manifested on earth as it is in heaven. The name of Jesus encapsulates the character, reputation, and essence of God Himself.

Operating in the name of Jesus goes beyond mere phonetics; it involves embodying the essence of the Person. Regrettably, some misuse the names Jesus, Yeshua, or Yahweh as if they were magical formulas, hoping for positive outcomes. However, those who invoke His name rightly are seeking His presence in a specific place. It is an act of summoning Him to that place.

Miracles occur and the will of God is fulfilled only when His presence or character is manifested. Those who embody the character of Christ become walking rebukes to the demonic kingdom and vessels through whom Christ is revealed in every circumstance.

The apostle Paul calls the character traits of Christ the "fruit of the Spirit." As he writes to the Galatians:

> The fruit of the Spirit is love, joy, peace, forbearance, kindness, goodness, faithfulness, gentleness and self-control. Against such things there is no law. Those who belong to Christ Jesus have crucified the flesh with its passions and desires. Since we live by the Spirit, let us keep in step with the Spirit (**Galatians 5:22-25, NIV**).

Notice that Paul uses the singular term "fruit" and not the plural "fruits." All of these character traits are intricately woven together. This "product" of the Spirit's character, though one, is nevertheless multi-dimensional in its manifestation.

These character traits are the *ways* of God. The Bible says that God "*made known his ways unto Moses, his acts unto the children of Israel*" (Psalm 103:7, KJV). In other words, the nation of Israel knew the actions of God—His miracles, signs, and wonders—but they did not know His ways. Moses knew God's ways. Early Christians were known as people of The Way, for they followed the One who said He was The Way. Many of us know the right thing to do, but we must learn to do the *right thing* the *right way*. We must have the ways of God formed within us. Only then can we accurately represent the heart and mind of God.

These character traits of Christ are also described as inner garments that we put on like clothing. Here again, we examine the words of the apostle Paul:

> *Therefore, as God's chosen people, holy and dearly loved, **clothe yourselves** with compassion, kindness, humility, gentleness and patience. Bear with each other and forgive one another if any of you has a grievance against someone. Forgive as the Lord forgave you. And over all these virtues **put on love**, which binds them all together in perfect unity* (**Colossians 3:12-14, NIV**).

We must daily "put on" these garments and clothe ourselves inwardly with Christ's character. This is one of the greatest benefits of our new life in Christ, and it sets us apart from all others who are still operating with the old Adamic nature. We have the opportunity to be clothed with the spiritual garments of Christ Jesus and to operate from the new nature.

The power of these various dimensions of Christ's essence cannot be overstated. For example, the unconditional, ever-enduring love of God is multi-directional in its expression, and it never fails. Paul writes:

> *I pray that out of his glorious riches he may strengthen you with power through his Spirit in your inner being, so that Christ may dwell in your hearts through faith. And I pray that you, being rooted and established in love, may have power, together with all the Lord's holy people, to grasp **how wide and long and high and deep is the love of Christ**, and to know this love that surpasses knowledge—that you*

may be filled to the measure of all the fullness of God (**Ephesians 3:16-19, NIV**).

What is meant by these four dimensions of the love of God?

The Width of God's Love

God's love is wide enough to accommodate all of us, no matter our background, upbringing, sins, failures, idiosyncrasies, and hangups.

The Length of God's Love

God's love will go the distance with us. He is there for the entire journey—start to finish—and He will see us through.

The Height of God's Love

God's love will lift us to incredibly high places in Him, beyond anything we could ask, think, or imagine.

The Depth of God's Love

God's love reaches down to the lowest possible place in order to find us and rescue us. No matter how far we descend, His love is deep enough to reach us, redeem us, and bring us higher.

It was this love that compelled God to offer His life for His creation, and it is this love that continues to reconcile that creation back to Him. If that is not a superpower, then I do not know what is. The character of God, by itself, is enough to

mark us as "enhanced human beings," but the grace and glory do not stop there. God also grants to us extraordinary, supernatural abilities that give expression to His sovereign power.

Gifts

> *God raised us up with Christ and seated us with him in the heavenly realms in Christ Jesus, in order that in the coming ages he might show the incomparable riches of his grace, expressed in his kindness to us in Christ Jesus* (**Ephesians 2:6-7, NIV**).

When we participate in Christ's ascension, we are given access to the spiritual gifts that God has allocated to us. Indeed, God *"has blessed us in the heavenly realms with every spiritual blessing in Christ"* (Ephesians 1:3, NIV).

Here are some of the spiritual gifts and abilities that are operative in the New Testament:[2]

Word of Wisdom

—the supernatural ability to discern the optimal course of action in any given situation

Word of Knowledge

—the supernatural ability to possess knowledge about people, places, and things without relying on conventional learning

Prophecy

—the supernatural ability to comprehend and articulate the mind of God on a given matter, providing insight into both the present and the future

Faith

—the supernatural ability to tap into and utilize the faith of Jesus Christ, trusting in divine realities

Healing

—the supernatural ability to receive cures from God and impart them to the sick

Miracles

—the supernatural ability to access the power of God, achieving feats that would otherwise be deemed impossible

Tongues

—the supernatural ability to speak known languages without conventional learning and to communicate with God through a heavenly language in prayer

Interpretation of Tongues

—the supernatural ability to interpret known languages without relying on conventional learning

Discerning of Spirits

—the supernatural ability to perceive and differentiate entities in the spiritual realm

Helps

—the supernatural ability to possess a diverse range of gifts to undergird/support the work of God

Administration

—the supernatural ability to coordinate people, systems, and resources for the implementation of the will of God

Serving

—the supernatural ability to selflessly contribute strategic labor for the fulfillment of needs and the advancement of the Kingdom

Teaching

—the supernatural ability to strengthen believers in their faith by comprehending, elucidating, and imparting profound truths

Encouragement

—the supernatural ability to instill courage, joy, comfort, and a divine perspective into every situation

Generosity (or Giving)

—the supernatural ability to willingly possess, steward, and properly distribute God's resources in the earth

Leadership

—the supernatural ability to influence, care, govern, and inspire confidence to the extent of creating devotees

Mercy

—the supernatural ability to significantly improve a person's life through genuine care, skill, and devotion

All of these gifts come from the Holy Spirit. Not everyone is given the same gifts, but we are all gifted, and we are also encouraged to *"eagerly desire the greater gifts"* (1 Corinthians 12:31, NIV). These special abilities are God's way of supernaturally enhancing us with His power.

Mantles

The grace to receive mantles is also found in the ascension of Christ. If the character traits of Christ serve as our "inner

garments," then mantles serve as our "outer garments." These are the specific "offices" to which we are called. When we receive a specific mantle from Christ, He anoints us and empowers us with authority in a position, and He graces us with the ability to complete an assignment.

The most prominent mantles are the ascension gifts:

- Apostles

- Prophets

- Evangelists

- Pastors

- Teachers

However, there are many mantles that we can receive in the ascension of Christ. We can receive mantles for the roles of husband, wife, mother, father, leader, worshiper, intercessor, businessperson, singer, writer, etc.

It is also possible to ask God for mantles that belonged to the faith giants of previous generations. The individual human beings may have transitioned to glory, but their mantles remain in the earth. When God told Elijah to anoint Elisha as a prophet in his stead, "*Elijah passed by him, and cast his mantle upon him*" (1 Kings 19:19, KJV). This symbolized what would eventually be the transfer of anointing, authority, and ability from Elijah to Elisha. The spiritual mantles that were worn by the great men and women of God in past millennia are still in the earth, and many of them are still available, waiting for someone to receive them from the Holy Spirit.

PUTTING THIS INTO PRACTICE

In the next chapter, we will empower you with several practical tools that you can put into practice on your journey toward enhanced humanity!

NOTES

1. Hugh D. Smith, *Co-Ruling with Christ: Practical Tools for Kingdom Dominion* (Independently published, 2022), 25.

2. See 1 Corinthians 12:4-11, 28; Romans 12:6-8; 1 Peter 4:10-11.

CHAPTER 5

HOW TO BECOME
AN ENHANCED HUMAN

THE ART OF SPIRITUAL CONCEPTION

After considering the character, gifts, and mantles that we can receive from the Holy Spirit, I cannot help but celebrate what God has done for us. What tremendous power we have access to in Christ! What authority! What ability! What capacity!

However, you may say, "All of this is great in theory, but how do I know what to receive from the Holy Spirit? How do I know what supernatural enhancements belong to me? And how do I actually receive them in my spirit?"

The first part of the answer, brothers and sisters, is to learn the art of spiritual conception. Through this practice, your spirit will conceive and become pregnant with the will of God. In natural human conception, a human seed fertilizes a human egg, which then becomes a zygote, an embryo, a fetus, and eventually, a fully matured and developed human being. The process of spiritual conception is analogous to this, as the faith-filled heart receives the seed of God's wisdom. Consider the art of spiritual conception:

1	Call on the Name of the Lord	Position and posture yourself before God, and petition Him on behalf of either yourself or another individual / community.
2	Offer God a Faith-Filled Heart	Sustain a believing heart before Him. Widely open your spirit in prayer. Trust Him, and prepare to receive from Him.
3	Receive the "Seed" of God	Receive the "download" of God from the heavens into your spirit, and experience spiritual conception.

The faith-filled heart of the believer serves as the "egg" that the "seed" of God fertilizes so that new life can be conceived. Consider the words of the apostle James:

> *If any of you lacks wisdom, you should ask God, who gives generously to all without finding fault, and it will be given to you. But when you ask, you must believe and not doubt, because the one who doubts is like a wave of the sea, blown and tossed by the wind. That person should not expect to receive anything from the Lord. Such a person is double-minded and unstable in all they do* **(James 1:5-8, NIV).**

When the believer offers God a faith-filled heart and receives His seed of wisdom, the believer becomes pregnant with the will of God, which can then be incubated in the soul and, if received as an act of intercession, imparted to others. The apostle James also instructs believers to "*receive with meekness the engrafted word, which is able to save your souls*" (James

1:21, KJV). That word *engrafted* also translates to "implanted." When we receive the seed of God's wisdom, we are essentially receiving a "Christ implant" that enhances us with supernatural power. In the same way that a person in need of a lung transplant can have their life extended by receiving a new lung, those who receive wisdom seeds become recipients of a Christ implant that will yield a special ability germane to the kind of wisdom received.

THE "WISDOM SEED" OF GOD

While the seed coat, embryo, and endosperm form the anatomical components of a typical plant seed, these individual parts do not encompass its complete narrative. As a product of reproduction, the seed inherently contains the genetic material, DNA, necessary for its full manifestation. Similar to a natural seed, the "wisdom seed" of God is packed with incredible potential. Wisdom is the ability to discern the optimal path toward achieving the highest objective in every situation. Wisdom inherently involves the skill to perceive the big picture—with each component in clear focus and in its rightful relation to the whole—in order to facilitate complete manifestation.

The potential of every wisdom seed resides within it, awaiting activation once it is planted. Indeed, a wisdom seed serves as the foundation of all created things. Rather than praying for specific material possessions like a house, car, food, clothing, career, or any creature comfort, one only needs to seek wisdom

from God. This wisdom seed has the capacity to produce all that is necessary.

However, the presence of wisdom in one area does not guarantee wisdom in all areas. I heard a story about a man on the continent of Africa who walked for three days to pray for a dead man, arriving with bloody feet because he carried his shoes to preserve them. Despite his faith and wisdom to raise the dead through the power of Jesus Christ, he lacked the wisdom to acquire the resources he needed for shoes. This illustrates how someone can be wise in one aspect but not in others. For instance, one may excel in business but struggle with interpersonal relationships—or be knowledgeable in astronomy and mathematics but lack in health management wisdom.

In Job 28:12-28 (NLT), we are provided with guidance on how and where to seek wisdom. Consider the elusive nature of wisdom as you read this passage:

> *But do people know where to find wisdom?*
> *Where can they find understanding?*
> *No one knows where to find it,*
> *for it is not found among the living.*
> *"It is not here," says the ocean.*
> *"Nor is it here," says the sea.*
> *It cannot be bought with gold.*
> *It cannot be purchased with silver.*
> *It's worth more than all the gold of Ophir,*
> *greater than precious onyx or lapis lazuli.*
> *Wisdom is more valuable than gold and crystal.*
> *It cannot be purchased with jewels mounted*
> *in fine gold.*
> *Coral and jasper are worthless in trying to get it.*

The price of wisdom is far above rubies.
Precious peridot from Ethiopia cannot be
exchanged for it.
It's worth more than the purest gold.

But do people know where to find wisdom?
Where can they find understanding?
It is hidden from the eyes of all humanity.
Even the sharp-eyed birds in the sky cannot
discover it.
Destruction and Death say,
"We've heard only rumors of where wisdom can be
found."

God alone understands the way to wisdom;
he knows where it can be found,
for he looks throughout the whole earth
and sees everything under the heavens.
He decided how hard the winds should blow
and how much rain should fall.
He made the laws for the rain
and laid out a path for the lightning.
Then he saw wisdom and evaluated it.
He set it in place and examined it thoroughly.
And this is what he says to all humanity:
"The fear of the Lord is true wisdom;
to forsake evil is real understanding."

APOSTOLIC INTERCESSION

The art of spiritual conception is one of the most powerful and effective ways to receive true wisdom and become a supernaturally enhanced human being (and to facilitate the enhancement of others). This practice is necessary for birthing God's will in our lives, families, and communities.

I also refer to this practice as *apostolic intercession*, for one of the primary tasks of an apostle, the first of the ascension gifts, is to experience spiritual conception on behalf of others. Apostles are called by God to equip the people of God and build up the Body of Christ until we reach maturity and fullness in Christ, and apostles are graced by God to identify deficiencies and to compensate for that which is lacking within individuals or communities. Apostles also build constructs within people that enhance and accelerate spiritual growth. This is accomplished, first and foremost, through apostolic intercession—or the art of spiritual conception.

The ascension gifts have a critically important role in facilitating the enhancement of God's people. The Kingdom of God has three branches of government: legislative, executive, and judicial. As the prophet Isaiah declared, "*the Lord is our judge, the Lord is our lawgiver, the Lord is our king; he will save us*" (Isaiah 33:22, KJV). The heavenly council operates as the legislative branch, and the court of Heaven operates as the judicial branch. The executive branch is facilitated, in part, by the ascension gifts in the Body of Christ. The apostle Paul highlights five prominent ascension gifts (also referred to as "five-fold ministry gifts") in his letter to the Ephesians:

*But to each one of us grace has been given as Christ apportioned it. This is why it says: "When he ascended on high, he took many captives and gave gifts to his people." (What does "he ascended" mean except that he also descended to the lower, earthly regions? He who descended is the very one who ascended higher than all the heavens, in order to fill the whole universe.) So Christ himself gave **the apostles, the prophets, the evangelists, the pastors and teachers**, to equip his people for works of service, so that the body of Christ may be built up until we all reach unity in the faith and in the knowledge of the Son of God and become mature, attaining to the whole measure of the fullness of Christ* (**Ephesians 4:7-13, NIV**).

In this time, it is absolutely imperative that all authentic apostles engage in apostolic intercession on behalf of God's people—to equip and enhance them with God's supernatural power.

I find myself praying night and day—seeking impartations or wisdom seeds from Christ on behalf of others—aiming to fill the gaps in their faith. On one occasion, after fervent prayer and receiving divine substance from Christ for an individual who was walking contrary to the things of God, I gladly imparted this new life to them. This impartation was accompanied by a prophetic utterance about their future, which they couldn't initially grasp. Over time, however, what seemed unrealistic and out of reach became a normal part of this person's life.

Apostolic and prophetic impartations serve to perfect that which is lacking in a person's faith, implant spiritual grace, and realign them with their true reality in God. The apostle

Paul wrote, *"Night and day we pray most earnestly that we may see you again and supply what is lacking in your faith"* (1 Thessalonians 3:10, NIV). The original apostles of the Lamb were deeply committed to apostolic intercession, prioritizing it above all other demands on their schedules.

I am convinced that apostles must operate in a manner similar to inventors and scientists, who must dedicate themselves to their pursuit so that the broader community can benefit from breakthrough insights and advancements. It was for this reason that the original apostles of the Lamb refused to allow anything to detract from the time they devoted to prayer. Significant, life-changing impartations occur only when apostles prioritize spending time with God, conceiving the necessary breakthroughs for others.

THE ART OF SPIRITUAL INCUBATION

In our day, human beings are attempting to enhance themselves by any means necessary. Some are pursuing this enhancement through science and technology. Others are embracing various "self-help" philosophies for behavior modification. Still others are even turning to witchcraft and other dark spiritual practices. But the supernatural enhancement that God has destined for humanity will only manifest through authentic deity activation. In other words, the Christ in us must be awakened, activated, and actualized.

Let me show you how this works. As we have stated, we must "put on" Christ so that we can experience the supernatural enhancement that comes from Him. Remember, we are

three-part beings—composed of spirit, soul, and body. Therefore, any supernatural enhancements that we wish to function with must be:

- *Received* in the spirit

- *Formed* in the soul

- *Expressed* in the body

Once spiritual conception takes place in the human spirit, the second part of the creative process involves incubation, or the formation of Christ within the human soul. After our spirits receive an enhancement from the Spirit of God, we must reprogram our souls to align with the new thing we have received from Him. Christ must be formed in our souls if He is to express Himself through our bodies.

Just as a human fetus experiences about nine months of incubation in the womb of its mother so that it can grow and develop properly before being birthed, the newly conceived will of God must be fully incubated within the human soul before being released. This incubation period allows the new life of God to experience a necessary stage of protected growth. During this period, we are being conformed to the image of Christ. All the parts of our spirit and soul (and, eventually, our body) are being internally aligned to the will of God, and we are becoming one with the Word.

Several practices that can assist us in this incubation process are:

- Christ-centered meditation

- Repetitive action

- Strategic experiences

- Fellowship

- Sacraments

- Co-laboring with Christ

- Anointed ministry

- Imprinting on someone who is following Christ

However, I would like to simplify the process even further by providing you with *the 10 steps to deity activation.*

THE 10 STEPS TO DEITY ACTIVATION

According to various New Testament passages, the Holy Spirit plays a crucial role in overseeing the affairs of the Church, guiding believers, revealing truth, showing future events, glorifying Jesus, providing comfort and advocacy, sanctifying and empowering, and teaching all things. While acknowledging the holiness of the Father's Spirit and recognizing that the Holy Spirit is the Spirit of Christ, it is essential to highlight the functional distinctions observed in the Holy Spirit's work within the New Testament Church.

One of the Holy Spirit's primary responsibilities is to unveil Jesus, the embodiment of Truth, to believers. This is accomplished by opening their spiritual eyes to perceive Jesus. Through deep communion, I often seek the Holy Spirit's guidance to reveal the resurrected Savior to me. This has led to

tremendous insight and understanding of many aspects of the living God.

Engaging in this practice has proven transformative, particularly during moments of ministry at the altar. The Holy Spirit grants prophetic insights when asked to reveal Christ Jesus, offering profound revelations about individuals. Asking the Holy Spirit to disclose Christ Jesus as the Healer has, on occasion, resulted in the transformative power of healing in someone's life.

Investing quality time in private communion with the Holy Spirit enhances the ability to perceive His work in public spaces. Requesting the Holy Spirit to reveal Christ Jesus emerges as the initial step in activating a connection with the divine nature.

Jesus said:

> *I have yet many things to say unto you, but ye cannot bear them now. Howbeit when he, the Spirit of truth, is come, he will guide you into all truth: for he shall not speak of himself; but whatsoever he shall hear, that shall he speak: and he will shew you things to come. He shall glorify me: for he shall receive of mine, and shall shew it unto you. All things that the Father hath are mine: therefore said I, that he shall take of mine, and shall shew it unto you* (**John 16:12-15, KJV**).

The initial moment of deity activation signifies the awakening of our born-again nature or divine DNA. This intrinsic divine DNA within every born-again believer's human spirit becomes operational when Christ is perceived. (Traditionally, Pentecostal groups, like the shakers and Quakers, have been

recognized for their physical responses to deity activation, marked by bodily vibrations or what some have culturally called a "quickening.")

It is my belief that the redemptive work of Christ goes far beyond behavior modification; it aims at deity activation. Christ's purpose is not merely to improve the old Adamic nature but to bring about new divine life.

Outlined here are the *10 steps to deity activation* which will assist believers in activating the divine DNA within their human spirit and forming it in their human soul. You will notice that Step 1 involves experiencing Christ through the guidance of the Holy Spirit, and Steps 2-10 correspond with the 9 parts of the soul discussed in the previous chapter. I encourage every believer to regularly put these 10 steps into practice:

1. "Holy Spirit, Show Me Jesus."

The first step is to commune with the Holy Spirit and ask Him to reveal Jesus to you.

2. Believe

Once Jesus is perceived through the Holy Spirit's revelation, you must then actively trust or believe what is being revealed to you. This allows the activated deity to begin to infiltrate the human soul. Sustained faith in this area will transform your *belief systems* and cause them to align with what the Holy Spirit is revealing to you.

3. Value

Next, actively value what is being revealed to you. Ascribe tremendous worth to the aspect of Christ that you are experiencing. This will affect your *values* and your priorities.

4. Accept

Fully accept and embrace the revelation. This will affect your *codes* and establish this new life of God as a personal law within your heart.

5. Honor

Honor this new life within your heart. This will set it as a new moral standard within you, affecting your *conscience*.

6. Emotionally Connect

Emotionally connecting to the revelation will transform your internal atmosphere. You must allow the experience to fill your *emotions*, as this is a particularly powerful way to allow it to sink deep within your heart.

7. Meditate

Focused, intentional meditation on what the Holy Spirit reveals will create new thought patterns within you, affecting the operation of your *intellect*.

8. Imagine

Imagine all the new possibilities associated with what you are experiencing in the Holy Spirit. This will establish a prophetic vision and activate your *imagination*.

9. Act

Acting upon the revelation will exercise your *will* and allow you to practice the principles that you have received. This solidifies the formation of Christ within the soul and leads to a new way of living.

10. Remember

Finally, choosing to remember the experience impacts your *memories* by creating a new personal history, a powerful tool in healing past traumas.

Full deity activation is only possible when the nine parts of the soul are impacted by the new life flowing from the divine DNA resident in the human spirit. If you practice this effectively in one area of revelation for 90 days, your life will never

be the same. You will be legitimately enhanced with the supernatural power of God.

THE POWER OF IMPARTATION

Once Christ is "formed" in us, we are ready to allow His power to flow through our physical bodies and impact the world around us. We are ready to train our bodies to align with what God has done in our spirits and souls, and we are ready to manifest His glory in the earth.

Notably, and powerfully, this new life from God can also be imparted to others. Consider this explanation of impartation from our previous book, *Co-Ruling with Christ*:

> Impartation is the transference of gifts from one person to another through the laying on of hands or other means. It involves the ability to give others that which God has allocated for them, and it rapidly accelerates spiritual growth. By receiving impartation, believers can experience a "quantum leap" in their spiritual journey as they learn from the Spirit of God in those with decades of experience. Ideally, growth by impartation should be a reality experienced by every single believer.
>
> Impartation is often related to "transfer of spirits." After Moses commissioned Joshua, his successor, to lead the children of Israel, it was said that "Joshua the son of Nun was full of the spirit of wisdom, for Moses had laid his hands on him" (Deuteronomy 34:9, ESV). Moses imparted a spirit of wisdom to Joshua

so that he could lead the people effectively. Similarly, the prophet Elisha, the protege of Elijah, received a "double portion" of Elijah's spirit.

The Apostle Paul said, "I long to see you so that I may impart to you some spiritual gift to make you strong" (Romans 1:11, NIV). We, too, should long to impart what God has allocated for other believers—and to receive impartation, as well.[1]

Not only can we become enhanced by the Holy Spirit, but we can also work with Him to enhance others around us. When fully activated, this supernatural enhancement will empower us to make the case to this generation that Jesus Christ is indeed Lord over all!

How does a spiritually enhanced human function?

They achieve mastery in utilizing their spiritual gifts and superpower, responding promptly to the Holy Spirit's directives while operating exclusively within the character of Christ. They collaborate with other spiritually empowered individuals, are missions minded, diligently pray for guidance, and they confront dark forces to establish God's Will.

Additionally, they evangelize, heal the sick, prophesy, perform miracles, and undertake any necessary action to make the case for the Lordship of Jesus Christ.

NOTE

1. Smith, *Co-Ruling with Christ*, 81.

CHAPTER 6

MAKING THE CASE
TO THIS GENERATION!

FOR SUCH A TIME AS THIS

We are living in a time unlike any other. Science and technology are advancing at an incredibly rapid pace. People are experimenting with and embracing all kinds of artificial human enhancements. Artificial intelligence is having a radical impact all around the globe. Our world is more globalized than ever before, and the risk of global pandemics is the highest it has ever been. Nations like China are rising and challenging the superpower status of the United States. Some are fearing a global economic collapse. Digital currencies are on the rise. Mental health crises are on the rise. Gender dysphoria is on the rise. Surveillance and government control are on the rise. Climate change is threatening our future. The antichrist agenda is stronger than ever. Some are even trying to ignite a clash of nations that will culminate in World War III.

It is in this context that we have been called to testify to our generation. Our ministry work today is to make the case for the Lordship of Jesus Christ and the efficacy of His redemptive justice work to individuals, families, and regions. We must

present compelling evidence to our world that Jesus is alive and that He reigns over all. This will require a demonstration of the Spirit's power like never before. Hear the words of the apostle Paul:

> *And so it was with me, brothers and sisters. When I came to you, I did not come with eloquence or human wisdom as I proclaimed to you the testimony about God. For I resolved to know nothing while I was with you except Jesus Christ and him crucified. I came to you in weakness with great fear and trembling. My message and my preaching were not with wise and persuasive words, but with a demonstration of the Spirit's power, so that your faith might not rest on human wisdom, but on God's power* (**1 Corinthians 2:1-5, NIV**).

Making the case for Christ in this generation will require more than wise and persuasive words. It will require supernaturally enhanced men and women of God who can demonstrate the authentic power of God in visible and tangible ways. And this is precisely what God is gracing us for. We have been called to the Kingdom for such a time as this, and the Holy Spirit is empowering us to become "superhuman" beings. The time is short, the stakes are high, and there is a clear sense of urgency. Just as God made Moses a god to Pharaoh, He is making us like gods in the earth to convince this generation of His Lordship.

A MORE POWERFUL TECHNOLOGY

Technological power and possibility are increasing at an exponential rate, and within the coming months and years, we are going to witness unprecedented levels of artificial human enhancements. Some of these technologies may be used for good purposes. Others will likely be weaponized in various ways.

However, the supernatural enhancement that we receive in Christ is far superior to any artificial enhancement that human beings can develop. The Kingdom technology that we have access to is far more powerful than any competing technologies in the systems of this world. It has always been this way, and it always will be. Consider again what happened when Moses and Aaron began to confront Pharaoh in Egypt:

> *The Lord said to Moses and Aaron, "When Pharaoh says to you, 'Perform a miracle,' then say to Aaron, 'Take your staff and throw it down before Pharaoh,' and it will become a snake."*
>
> *So Moses and Aaron went to Pharaoh and did just as the Lord commanded. Aaron threw his staff down in front of Pharaoh and his officials, and it became a snake. Pharaoh then summoned wise men and sorcerers, and the Egyptian magicians also did the same things by their secret arts: Each one threw down his staff and it became a snake. But Aaron's staff swallowed up their staffs* (**Exodus 7:8-12, NIV**).

Though Pharaoh's sorcerers had the ability to "perform miracles" in a way that mimicked the power of God, their staffs were

ultimately swallowed by Aaron's staff. The wisdom from above proved superior to the wisdom from beneath. And eventually, as the plagues on Egypt continued, the power of God went beyond anything that could even be mimicked by the Egyptian sorcerers, at which point they admitted: *"This is the finger of God"* (Exodus 8:19, NIV). The supernatural enhancement that we experience in Christ will enable us to display God's power in ways that will unequivocally testify to this generation that Jesus is Lord of all.

In Zechariah 1, the prophet received a vision of four horns that scattered Judah, Israel, and Jerusalem. But then the prophet saw four craftsmen who would terrify and throw down the four horns of the nations. There are many "horns" that have raised themselves up in our time: sickness and disease, poverty, corruption, family malfunction, war, etc. But God is raising up the craftsmen—supernaturally enhanced humans who have been trained to skillfully use Kingdom technologies. These masters of "Christ craft" will be empowered to work miracles and demonstrate the power of God in unmistakable ways.

THE MARK OF THE BEAST?

The book of Revelation foretells of a time when a wicked world leader will arise, deceiving the entire world through mystifying miracles and the creation of an image that appears to possess life. While history has seen many antichrist figures, this particular one will surpass them all in evil and power. Granted authority to dominate the earth, he will perform unimaginable deeds for a season—demanding worship and unwavering

allegiance to himself and his system, under threat of death. Utilizing technology, he will wield global surveillance capabilities and mark all citizens of his kingdom with an implant or something comparable.

Then I saw another beast come up out of the earth. He had two horns like those of a lamb, but he spoke with the voice of a dragon. He exercised all the authority of the first beast. And he required all the earth and its people to worship the first beast, whose fatal wound had been healed. He did astounding miracles, even making fire flash down to earth from the sky while everyone was watching. And with all the miracles he was allowed to perform on behalf of the first beast, he deceived all the people who belong to this world. He ordered the people to make a great statue of the first beast, who was fatally wounded and then came back to life. He was then permitted to give life to this statue so that it could speak. Then the statue of the beast commanded that anyone refusing to worship it must die.

He required everyone—small and great, rich and poor, free and slave—to be given a mark on the right hand or on the forehead. And no one could buy or sell anything without that mark, which was either the name of the beast or the number representing his name. Wisdom is needed here. Let the one with understanding solve the meaning of the number of the beast, for it is the number of a man. His number is 666 (**Revelation 13:11-18, NLT**).

This mark acts as a seal for the followers of the antichrist and the false prophet (the spokesperson for the antichrist). The false prophet (the second beast) is the one who causes people to take this mark, which is literally placed in the hand or forehead.

Recent advancements in medical implant chip and RFID (Radio-Frequency Identification) technologies have sparked renewed interest in the mark of the beast mentioned in Revelation 13. It is conceivable that the technologies we are witnessing today may signify the initial stages of what could eventually be utilized as the mark of the beast. The medical implant chip and other technologies in use today appear to be precursors to the actual rollout of this demonic system.

The mark of the beast will be bestowed exclusively upon those who worship the antichrist. Simply having a medical or financial microchip inserted into one's right hand or forehead does not constitute the mark of the beast. Instead, the mark of the beast will be an end-times identification mandated by the antichrist for conducting transactions, and it will be issued only to those who pledge allegiance to him.

Many reputable scholars of Revelation hold divergent views on the precise nature of the mark of the beast. Besides the implanted chip theory, other conjectures include an ID card, a microchip, a barcode tattooed into the skin, or simply a mark signifying allegiance to the antichrist's kingdom. Essentially, present and emerging technologies make any of these interpretations plausible.

Similarly, the meaning of 666 remains a mystery. In Revelation 13, the number 666 identifies a person, and the passage clearly indicates that wisdom is needed to understand and

calculate the number of the beast. Thus, somehow the number 666 is the number of a man, and it will serve to identify the antichrist. Throughout the centuries, scholars have attempted to associate certain individuals with 666, yet no conclusive identification has been made. That is why Revelation 13:18 emphasizes the need for wisdom. When the antichrist is revealed (see 2 Thessalonians 2:3-4), his identity and the significance of the number 666 will become clear.

TESTIFY TO THE TRUTH!

As believers, we know that we overcome by the blood of the Lamb and by the word of our testimony (see Revelation 12:11). We also know that *the testimony of Jesus is the spirit of prophecy*" (Revelation 19:10, ESV). We speak often about being witnesses for Christ, presenting our testimonies, and testifying to the truth. These terms that we employ—*witness, testimony, testify*—are all legal terms. It is as if we are in a grand courtroom and we have been called to the witness stand to provide eyewitness testimony that provides sufficient evidence to render a verdict in a case. Our lives are intended to provide compelling evidence to the world around us that Jesus is alive and that He is Lord of all. Therefore, we must testify to the truth of Jesus Christ—by our words, by our deeds, and by our lives—so that the world can see Him for who He is.

We must ask ourselves, "Who am I in Christ? And who is Christ in me?" Each of us represents a specific revelation of the nature and character of Christ. God has shaped our lives and identities in such a way that we would each reveal a unique

aspect of His Person. Christ intends to live His life through us, and He desires that His grace would work in us mightily to that end. This means that our lives are not our own. We exist to reveal Christ.

There is a heavenly script that contains all of God's predetermined counsel concerning our lives, and each of us is living out a "chapter" of Christ from that script. The writer of Hebrews makes clear that even Jesus Himself came to fulfill what was written of Him:

> Then I said, "Behold, I have come—In the volume of the book it is written of Me—To do Your will, O God" (Hebrews 10:7, NKJV).

In the Old Testament, many of the patriarchs, prophets, priests, and kings were "types" of Christ. In other words, their lives foreshadowed Christ in various ways. They had to have certain experiences, say certain words, and execute specific actions because their lives were serving as prophetic pictures of the Messiah who was to come. And when Jesus came, He fulfilled all of the "types and shadows" of the Old Testament through his birth, life, death, burial, resurrection, ascension, and reign.

As New Testament believers, we are called by God not to be types, but to be testimonies. We are no longer foreshadowing Christ; we are expressing His glory in the earth. Through our lives, we are bearing witness to the risen Lord. Therefore, we must be accurate and precise in our representation of Him, for we are functioning as His ambassadors to the world.

Consider the two witnesses found in Revelation 11:1-13. They were empowered by the Holy Spirit to prophesy in the

city of Jerusalem for 1,260 days, confirming their words with powerful signs and wonders. They were testifying to the truth of Jesus, and upon completing their testimony, they were killed. Their completed testimony triggered a divine verdict, a judgment from the heavens, and they themselves were resurrected and vindicated.

This text emphasizes that our purpose as believers is to reveal the living Christ through Spirit-inspired words and deeds. Our genuine testimonies, once completed, will trigger verdicts from the heavenly Judge. These verdicts will approve and advance those who have received the testimony, and they will penalize those who have rejected the testimony.

The Church's power lies in provoking divine judgment on regions, cities, and even nations by completing authentic testimonies. While we do not agree with the "hyper Kingdom movement" that suggests that the Church will take over the world prior to the return of Christ, we do believe that we have been called to powerfully influence the world and prompt divine judgments. In this way, we will fulfill our dominion mandate until the Second Coming of Christ. Lord Jesus, grant us grace to fulfill what You have written about us from the heavens!

The Lord revealed to me that many believers in this season will be sent to individuals, families, communities, and even nations to testify about different aspects of Christ. Some may be sent to a community for two years to reveal God's love, while others may be tasked with demonstrating the power of Christ to an individual for 30 days. Another may be sent to a city for 10 years to reveal God's wisdom. These testimonies are intended to advance and bless.

However, unfortunately, many of God's witnesses are rejected, and their testimonies become evidence of hard hearts and rejection of God. Therefore, God will render a verdict from heaven, either advancing and approving those who receive the testimony or penalizing those who reject it. Just as godly people in past generations have shaken nations and cities through their testimonies, we are poised to do the same in this time. Therefore, we must not allow anything to compromise our testimony, for it is the only way to invoke a verdict from heaven and a true move of God on earth.

Over the years, I have learned that God will use the context in which a person exists as a courtroom for them to testify or reveal Christ. Consider the last book of the Bible, the Revelation of Jesus Christ. While some may view it solely as a depiction of apocalyptic and frightening events, it goes beyond that. It reveals Christ in some of the most bizarre and unusual situations, affirming that Christ is intended to be revealed in all facets of life, as He is all in all. Therefore, we should no longer fear difficult, bizarre, or tragic events, as God has chosen all of them as platforms for disciples to reveal Christ.

A testimony is not restricted to what God has done for us but also what He is doing through us by Christ. The moment we overcome our fear of difficult and tragic circumstances, we can confidently testify about Christ in any situation or state we find ourselves in. Remember, once the testimonies are complete, a divine verdict will follow, either advancing those who received the testimony or penalizing those who rejected it. Jesus even instructed His disciples to wipe the dust off their feet as a testimony against those who rejected His message.

True testimonies always shake environments when they are complete. After the apostle Paul finished his testimony in the

Philippian jail, there was a tremendous earthquake. After the two witnesses in Revelation 11 finished their testimony, an earthquake ensued, and after our Lord Jesus finished His testimony on the cross, there was a tremendous earthquake.

We must not allow the enemy of our faith to compromise our testimony, rendering us unbelievable and inconsequential to the things of God. Let us solely rely on the Holy Spirit to empower us to be His witnesses—providing infallible proof of His life and lordship in every place we are sent!

A PECULIAR PEOPLE

Many of us may be familiar with the verse of Scripture that says we are "*a chosen generation, a royal priesthood, an holy nation, a peculiar people*" (1 Peter 2:9, KJV). However, that word *peculiar* does not mean "strange." In the original Greek language, it actually means that we are God's acquired possession. We are His special treasure.

In that sense, we are like God's pocket change, and He is able to "spend" us to "purchase" certain things in the earth. All unjust suffering is redemptive, and through His death on the cross, Jesus Christ purchased the salvation of the world. However, we as Christ's Body are also called to fill up "*what is lacking in the afflictions of Christ*" (Colossians 1:24, NKJV). In other words, we are called to be partakers of Christ's suffering, and therefore, we allow Him to "spend" our lives to make some big things happen.

Like the apostle Paul commanded Timothy, we must make "*full proof*" of our ministry, and like the apostle Paul himself,

we must fight a good fight, finish our course, and keep the faith (2 Timothy 4:5,7, KJV). We must love not our lives unto the death so that the world can see Jesus!

PRACTICING REDEMPTIVE JUSTICE

The Holy Spirit is enhancing and empowering the Church to establish the Kingdom of God on earth as it is in heaven. But how will this happen? The Kingdom will come to earth when we use our Spirit-given enhancements to practice redemptive justice. Virtually every human being has some innate sense of justice, but human "justice" can take on many different forms. For example:

Retributive Justice

This form of justice involves the punishment of individuals who have violated laws and committed wrongful acts, and it aims to achieve vengeance and deter others from following a similar path.

Restorative Justice

This form of justice focuses on the rehabilitation of offenders through reconciliation with victims and the community at large.

Distributive Justice

This form of justice strives for the fair allocation of resources and benefits in society, ensuring that individuals receive their fair share based on principles of equity and need. (*Equity* means that one's rewards and benefits are equal to one's contributions and capacity. *Equality* means that everyone gets the same amount, regardless of input.)

Procedural Justice

This form of justice refers to the idea of fairness in the processes that resolve disputes and how people's perceptions of fairness are strongly impacted by the quality of their experiences.

By contrast, the practice of redemptive justice is rooted in the application of the finished work of Christ, and it is modeled after God's balanced nature and His original intent for human beings to live in harmony with Him and with one another. Redemptive justice is built upon the foundation of Christ, and it reflects God's loving heart for His creation. It transcends the forms of justice mentioned above because it both encompasses them and goes beyond them, and it brings the highest and most righteous Judge to every situation by activating His redemptive work.

God was willing to spare the twin cities of Sodom and Gomorrah if there were only 50 righteous people in the city. Unfortunately, there were not enough righteous individuals. Abraham persisted in his intercession before God to spare the city, asking God to save it if there were 40 righteous, then

30, followed by 20, and finally concluding with only 10. God agreed to spare the city if there were only 10 righteous people.

Tzedakah is a Hebrew word that means justice and righteousness, and it refers to the just and righteous acts that restore balance in any situation. God was willing to spare an entire city from impending judgment if only 10 people were present to do justice. In this season, those who are empowered with the ability to do justice will be used by God to save cities from judgment. *"Righteousness exalts a nation, but sin is a reproach to any people"* (Proverbs 14:34, ESV).

We know from Scripture how important justice is to God:

> But let justice roll on like a river, righteousness like a never-failing stream! (**Amos 5:24, NIV**)

> The Lord loves righteousness and justice; the earth is full of his unfailing love (**Psalm 33:5, NIV**).

> Blessed are those who act justly, who always do what is right (**Psalm 106:3, NIV**).

> The God of Israel said, the Rock of Israel spoke to me: "He who rules over men must be just, ruling in the fear of God" (**2 Samuel 23:3, NKJV**).

> The Lord said, "Shall I hide from Abraham what I am about to do, seeing that Abraham shall surely become a great and mighty nation, and all the nations of the earth shall be blessed in him? For I have chosen him, that he may command his children and his household after him to keep the way of the Lord by doing righteousness and justice, so that the Lord may bring

to Abraham what he has promised him" (**Genesis 18:17-19, ESV**).

The biblical idea of justice ultimately reflects God's loving intent for His creation and His desire to bring that creation back into a state of *shalom*—His harmonious, synergistic, productive, supernatural peace and wellness. Our God is a God of balance, and His justice restores balance to individuals, families, communities, regions, and nations.

Redemptive justice involves ascertaining the heart and mind of God at these various levels and manifesting what He has decreed from the heavens. This will often necessitate engaging in high-level spiritual warfare with demonic entities in order to usher in God's Kingdom of righteousness, peace, and joy.

CONDUCTING SPIRITUAL WARFARE CAMPAIGNS

God administers His justice by means of His spiritual covering—represented by His government, including His heavenly council. God's covering is designed to protect, nurture, and bless all who are in covenant relationship with Him. To this end, the Bible is replete with evidence that God convenes gatherings of heavenly beings that He commissions to attend to Him, deliberate with Him, and execute His will. Here are just a few examples:

> *The heavens praise your wonders, Lord, your faithfulness too, in the assembly of the holy ones. For who in the skies above can compare with the Lord? Who is like the Lord among the heavenly beings? In the*

council of the holy ones God is greatly feared; he is more awesome than all who surround him (**Psalm 89:5-7, NIV**).

God has taken his place in the divine council; in the midst of the gods he holds judgment (**Psalm 82:1, ESV**)

And Micaiah said, "Therefore hear the word of the Lord: I saw the Lord sitting on his throne, and all the host of heaven standing beside him on his right hand and on his left" (**1 Kings 22:19, ESV**).

You are the Lord, you alone. You have made heaven, the heaven of heavens, with all their host, the earth and all that is on it, the seas and all that is in them; and you preserve all of them; and the host of heaven worships you (**Nehemiah 9:6, ESV**).

The sentence is by the decree of the watchers, the decision by the word of the holy ones, to the end that the living may know that the Most High rules the kingdom of men and gives it to whom he will and sets over it the lowliest of men (**Daniel 4:17, ESV**).

Now there was a day when the sons of God came to present themselves before the Lord, and Satan also came among them (**Job 1:6, ESV**).

We have also noted that God assigned angelic coverings to the nations of the earth: "*When the Most High assigned lands to the nations, when he divided up the human race, he established the boundaries of the peoples according to the number*

in his heavenly court" (Deuteronomy 32:8, NLT). Daniel 10 specifically mentions angels who were assigned to Israel, Persia, and Greece. Of course, many of these angelic entities are now fallen, demonic spirits that are actively rebelling against God and exerting their negative influence over various people groups around the world.

Just as individual human beings are composed of spirits, souls, and bodies, so cities—and even nations—have collective spirits, souls, and bodies. The spirit of a community can consist of the Holy Spirit, holy angels, and the collective essence of agreeable human spirits that reside in the community. Alternatively, the spirit of a community can consist of the covering principality, demonic spirits, and the collective essence of agreeable human spirits that reside in the community.

In this sense, the Bible can speak of the spiritual health or spiritual corruption of a city, nation, or people group. For example, Jerusalem, though it was once called the City of Peace, is spiritually called Sodom and Egypt later in the text: "*And their dead bodies shall lie in the street of the great city, which spiritually is called Sodom and Egypt, where also our Lord was crucified*" (Revelation 11:8, KJV).

The soul of a city comprises its institutions and culture. The concept of a city having a soul was introduced by Plato in *The Republic*, where he posited that the state is infused with a soul resembling that of an individual person. He asked, "Must we not acknowledge that in each of us there are the same principles and habits which there are in the state; and that from the individual they pass into the state?"

The body of a city consists of its geography, buildings, minerals, crime rates, state of human resources, and all visible

assets and liabilities. The body reflects the condition of both the spirit and soul of the city.

Once again, redemptive justice is the divine work of bringing balance to individuals, cities, and nations through righteous acts inspired by Christ. In future writings, I intend to delve deeper into this subject. For now, consider Alice Bailey's work as one reason why the redemption of the spirit and soul of a nation is necessary. Alice Bailey (1880–1949) was one of the founders of the New Age movement, and she is known for coining the term "New Age" in her writings, which mostly focus on the subject of theosophy.

Britannica describes theosophy as an "occult movement originating in the 19th century with roots that can be traced to ancient Gnosticism and Neoplatonism. The term *theosophy*, derived from the Greek *theos* ('god') and *sophia* ('wisdom'), is generally understood to mean 'divine wisdom.'"[1] Alice Bailey claimed that the majority of her work was telepathically dictated to her by a so-called "Master of Wisdom" or spirit entity identified as Djwal Khul.

Many believe that Alice Bailey's 10-Point Plan is part of a larger strategy to eventually introduce a New World Order system. The 10-Point Plan is as follows:

1. Take God and prayer out of the education system.

2. Reduce parental authority over children.

3. Destroy the Judeo-Christian family structure or the traditional Christian family structure.

4. If sex is free, then make abortion legal and make it easy.

5. Make divorce easy and legal; free people from the concept of marriage for life.

6. Make homosexuality an alternative lifestyle.

7. Debase art; make it run mad.

8. Use media to promote and change mindsets.

9. Create an interfaith movement.

10. Get governments to make all these law, and get the Church to endorse these changes.

Since principalities and other demonic entities can become the spiritual "covering" over a city, and since it is God's desire that His Kingdom come on earth as it is in heaven, God's people are called to engage in spiritual warfare—not just at the individual deliverance level, but at the collective community level. It is the Church's responsibility to displace demonic power and establish the government of God. God will not allow injustice to continue always. He will address it, and He will make things right. Consider Psalm 2 (NKJV):

Why do the nations rage,
And the people plot a vain thing?
The kings of the earth set themselves,
And the rulers take counsel together,
Against the Lord and against His Anointed, saying,
"Let us break Their bonds in pieces
And cast away Their cords from us."

He who sits in the heavens shall laugh;
The Lord shall hold them in derision.

Then He shall speak to them in His wrath,
And distress them in His deep displeasure:
"Yet I have set My King
On My holy hill of Zion."

I will declare the decree:
The Lord has said to Me,
"You are My Son,
Today I have begotten You.
Ask of Me, and I will give You
The nations for Your inheritance,
And the ends of the earth for Your possession.
You shall break them with a rod of iron;
You shall dash them to pieces like a potter's vessel."

Now therefore, be wise, O kings;
Be instructed, you judges of the earth.
Serve the Lord with fear,
And rejoice with trembling.
Kiss the Son, lest He be angry,
And you perish in the way,
When His wrath is kindled but a little.
Blessed are all those who put their trust in Him.

We are called to partner with God in the displacement of demonic power and the advancement of the government of God, for *"we wrestle not against flesh and blood, but against principalities, against powers, against the rulers of the darkness of this world, against spiritual wickedness in high places"* (Ephesians 6:12, KJV). Although this is not primarily a book about spiritual warfare, and though we do not have the opportunity in this context to give the subject its full treatment, it is

important that we understand a few high-level guidelines for spiritual warfare at the city level:

1. Devote time to intentional prayer and spiritual mapping of the city.

2. Discover the true prophetic vision of the city. Prophetic vision consists of the following:

    a. Divine Decree

    b. Divine Allocation

    c. Divine Promises

    d. Divine Blessings

3. Discover the perverse vision of the city. Perverse vision consists of the following:

    a. Demonic Decree

    b. Demonic Allocation

    c. Demonic Promises

    d. Demonic Curses

4. Use the prophetic vision to both plan and conduct a spiritual warfare campaign. The primary purpose of this campaign is to open and sustain Kingdom "portals" and to neutralize or sever the links to demonic entities and ruling human spirits.

A spiritual warfare campaign may include the following elements:

- Vows made to God

- Confession of the prophetic vision

- Declaration of the prophetic vision

- The identification of targets

- Divine renouncements

- Divine wrath of God (the death of Christ)

- Divine purification (the burial of Christ)

- Divine resurrection power (the resurrection of Christ)

- Angelic support

- An appointed presbytery to establish the prophetic vision and open/sustain Kingdom portals

GOD'S VISION FOR HUMAN SOCIETY

The ultimate prophetic vision for human society is New Jerusalem, the Garden-City described in the book of Revelation, where heaven and earth perfectly overlap. Consider this utopian reality that God intends for His people:

Then I saw "a new heaven and a new earth," for the first heaven and the first earth had passed away, and there was no longer any sea. I saw the Holy City, the new Jerusalem, coming down out of heaven from God, prepared as a bride beautifully dressed for her husband. And I heard a loud voice from the throne saying, "Look! God's dwelling place is now among the people, and he will dwell with them. They will be his people, and God himself will be with them and be their God. 'He will wipe every tear from their eyes. There will be no more death' or mourning or crying or pain, for the old order of things has passed away" **(Revelation 21:1-4, NIV).**

I did not see a temple in the city, because the Lord God Almighty and the Lamb are its temple. The city does not need the sun or the moon to shine on it, for the glory of God gives it light, and the Lamb is its lamp. The nations will walk by its light, and the kings of the earth will bring their splendor into it. On no day will its gates ever be shut, for there will be no night there. The glory and honor of the nations will be brought into it. Nothing impure will ever enter it, nor will anyone who does what is shameful or deceitful, but only those whose names are written in the Lamb's book of life **(Revelation 21:22-27, NIV).**

Then the angel showed me the river of the water of life, as clear as crystal, flowing from the throne of God and of the Lamb down the middle of the great street of the city. On each side of the river stood the tree of life, bearing twelve crops of fruit, yielding its

fruit every month. And the leaves of the tree are for the healing of the nations. No longer will there be any curse. The throne of God and of the Lamb will be in the city, and his servants will serve him. They will see his face, and his name will be on their foreheads. There will be no more night. They will not need the light of a lamp or the light of the sun, for the Lord God will give them light. And they will reign for ever and ever (**Revelation 22:1-5, NIV**).

What a powerful and moving vision! One day, all the kingdoms of this earth will become the Kingdom of God. One day, all the swords will be beaten into plowshares. One day, every knee will bow and every tongue will confess that He is Lord. One day, God will be all in all. And that day is getting closer and closer. In fact, I believe that we are now at the beginning stages of a Kingdom Renaissance that will eventually culminate with the Second Coming of Christ.

KINGDOM RENAISSANCE

Over a year ago, as of this writing, the Lord told me that we had entered the beginning stages of a Kingdom Renaissance. The word *renaissance* means "rebirth," and this Kingdom Renaissance would be a rebirth of authentic Kingdom culture in the earth.

Historically, the European Renaissance was the period immediately following the Middle Ages, and it was characterized by a resurgence of classical scholarship, geographical

exploration, advancements in astronomy, new inventions and innovations, and a revival of art and literature. This intellectual and artistic explosion brought Europe out of what some have called the "Dark Ages," and some have also suggested that it led to the Protestant Reformation.

The Lord showed me that the Kingdom Renaissance would have several characteristics, including (but not limited to) the following:

- God working powerfully in Generation Z and Generation Alpha, shattering what some might call "age-appropriate restrictions"

- The return of men to the Church and the restoration of biblical masculinity

- The restoration of true brotherhood and sisterhood through genuine covenant relationships

- Authentic deliverance

- The restoration of evangelism and soul-winning, culminating in a great end-time harvest of souls

- Authentic apostolic and prophetic gifts

- Believers operating with the gifts of the Spirit and the fruit of the Spirit

- Property ownership

- The restoration of the fear of the Lord and reverence for the Church

- Strong families led by strong parents

- Distinctions between holy and unholy, clean and unclean

- Heightened spiritual, intellectual, artistic, and social activity that will bring about new things in the Kingdom of God

Ultimately, the Kingdom Renaissance will involve the rediscovery and implementation of the *ways* of God in every area of human life and culture.

Brothers and sisters, we have now entered the Golden Era of the Kingdom of God, heralding the rebirth of true Kingdom culture. We stand on the precipice of a period destined to last until the return of our Lord. It marks the beginning of a glorious Church, where His glory and power will rest upon us in unprecedented ways, steadily increasing until the day our Lord returns and establishes His Kingdom on Earth in fullness.

THE TIME IS **NOW!**

Dr. Martin Luther King Jr. spoke of "the fierce urgency of now." I have been in ministry for 36 years, and there is an unprecedented, unmistakable sense of urgency in my spirit right now. God is moving at a rapid pace, and He is demanding more of those in leadership during this time. We must receive supernatural human enhancement, and we must facilitate the enhancement of those around us. Forces are amassing, powers are posturing themselves, the times are accelerating, and the stakes are incredibly high. A clash of kingdoms is imminent,

and we must be fully equipped and prepared for what is already here and what is soon coming.

My prayer is that you would employ the principles and practices in this book and that you would allow the Holy Spirit to supernaturally enhance you for the work of His Kingdom in this hour. May you be spiritually augmented by the power of God. May you become all of who you were born to be. May you receive every character trait, gift, and mantle that God has allocated for you. May you embrace your identity, purpose, and calling in Christ. May you demonstrate the supernatural authority and ability of God through words, deeds, miracles, signs, and wonders. May you testify to this generation that Jesus is alive and that He is Lord of all, and may your completed testimony trigger a verdict from the heavenly Judge that will radically shift people, families, cities, regions, and nations. May you partner with ascension gifts in the Body of Christ to displace demonic powers and usher in the Kingdom of God—a Kingdom of righteousness, peace, and joy. And may your witness to the risen Lord reverberate through the heavens forever!

NOTE

1. J. Gordon Melton, *Encyclopedia Britannica*, s.v. "theosophy," February 22, 2024, https://www.britannica.com/topic/theosophy.

ABOUT
THE AUTHOR

Hugh Daniel Smith is a multidimensional thinker and international speaker. He is known for his spiritual insights and ability to make them relevant to the times. His life's mission is to bring the Kingdom of God to earth by protecting the divine rights of all people. His unique style, charismatic wit, godly wisdom, and genuine love for people have been indispensable to his success.

ENDORSEMENTS

As I dove into *Higher Authority* by my brother, Bishop Hugh Smith Jr., I felt a surge of pride. Growing up, Hugh mirrored the adventurous spirit of the *Lost in Space* episode "Danger, Will Robinson," always daring to explore the unknown. Hugh fearlessly explores the divine mandate for human evolution, seamlessly blending scripture, science, and spirituality.

Dr. Tino W. Smith

We are once again inundated by the wealth of knowledge and applicable truths from the intellectual mind of Hugh Daniel Smith Jr. as he guides us through God's plan and pattern for human enhancement!

Bishop Roderick Roberts